FOLLOW *the* LEADER

JYOTIKA HAYNES

ISBN: 978-1-957203-44-7 (sc)
ISBN: 978-1-957203-45-4 (hc)
ISBN: 978-1-957203-46-1 (e)

THE EWINGS PUBLISHING

The Ewings Publishing LLC
One Galleria Blvd., Suite 1900, Metairie, LA 70001
1-888-421-2397

Contents

Chapter One

OUR SOUL'S SOLE PURPOSE: OUR JOURNEY THROUGH THIS LIFETIME

My paternal grandfather was a deeply spiritual man.

He was a train driver in Jhansi, driving passenger trains that carried hundreds of people to different places in India. On one trip, through the jungles at night, he was overcome with an eerie feeling that something was terribly wrong.

He instructed his fireman to check everything in the engine – only to be told everything was operating, "just fine."

The uneasy feeling persisted and then he saw a red light, way out in front of him; someone was waving a kerosene lantern in the distance.

He anxiously called out to his fireman to have a look outside, but his fireman saw only the darkness of the night. But to grandfather's eyes the lantern was now being waved at a frantic pace, back and forth. He felt he had to stop the train by applying the brake and slowly the train came to a halt. The guard, including many sleepy passengers were annoyed my grandfather had stopped the train and wanted an explanation. Although the red light was no longer there, he explained to all what his eyes had seen.

The passengers were asked to get back onto the train, the guard returned to his carriage and whilst the fireman cranked up the engine, my grandfather took the opportunity to walk further along the track.

The nagging feeling was still within him, so he continued walking 'til he came to the bridge only to find that it was no longer there. It had been completely washed away by the flooded river.

The railway line his train was on came abruptly to an end.

Had grandfather ignored the red light, not taken that walk, and not listened to his innermost feelings, the speed that crowded train was travelling at would not have given him any time to stop when he approached the washed away bridge.

No one on that train questioned my grandfather. For them it was a miracle, their lives had been spared because one person listened to his inner voice.

Most people will openly acknowledge that, along with being human beings, we are also spiritual beings, but they know little of their spiritual nature.

Today we have much knowledge and information about the human body. We know that if we eat certain foods our body will stay healthy; that exercise is good for our bodies and that too much exposure to the sun is harmful to our body.

We are blessed with schools, colleges, and a vast assortment of teaching resources to extend and stimulate our intellectual mind. Most people today have some type of formal education. There are also psychiatrists, psychologists, and therapists to help us understand and deal with our emotional issues.

But little is being done about our spiritual growth.

What about the understanding and nurturing of our soul?

We have become so preoccupied with our body that our spiritual growth has been neglected, or worse still, ignored. Many people are embarrassed by talk of spiritually.

I remember a few years back, I was alone one night and awoke suddenly to find my bedroom filled with a brilliant light, impossible to describe, amazingly, it did not hurt my eyes.

In my half-awake state, I thought the TV had come on – no and neither were any lights on.

Then I realised that it was from elsewhere, and as the light vanished, I was left breathless and in a state of awe and wonder.

For the next couple of days, I must have been on what I can only describe as a spiritual high because I felt elated, incredibly light.

Even today the memory of that incident is so strong I can recall it with total clarity.

My mentioning this to a very few close family members was a mistake as they were totally uncomfortable with it and dismissed it as a figment of my imagination.

We come here from the spirit world, when we die, we will return to it.

Einstein said, 'the intuitive mind is a sacred gift, and the rational mind is a faithful servant.

We have created a society that honours the servant and has forgotten the gift.'

My grandfather had used both his rational and his intuitive mind. His training as an engine driver allowed him to physically slow down and stop the train, thereby saving a lot of people from imminent death. When human resources failed him, subsequent authorities were unaware that the floods had destroyed the bridge he was able to tap into his spiritual resources.

When we combine our spiritual nature with our human nature, we reach our fullest potential, and this leads to self-realization.

Our sole purpose for being here is to develop our souls; and this can only be done when we consciously change all those negative traits of our inherited and conditioned personality by controlling the mind using the spiritual energy from within. This energy gives us the willpower to resist and control the weaker aspects of our human nature and allows our thoughts and actions to be guided by our higher Self.

When we make a conscious effort to change our human nature for a more spiritual nature through meditation and contemplation, the divine energy that permeates all of space, will flow freely through us.

Remember, God will help those who help themselves.

This divine energy will bring our body, mind, and soul together in total harmony to reflect a pure personality of a true enlightened being and we will become one with the Divine.

Hanuman, from Hindu sacred text whom scholars believe to be the first recorded anthropoid man an Ape most resembling man, told Lord Rama,

"Oh Lord, while I identify myself with my body, I am thy servant.
When I consider myself an individual soul, I am thy part.
When I look upon myself as the spirit, I am one with thee."
And words spoken by Jesus before his death upon the cross were:
"Father into thy hands I commit my spirit."

This is the evolution of the Soul, and this is our purpose for being here – to become one with the Divine.

But getting there is the difficult task.

There is a story of an elderly illiterate man asking a young scholar to read a map for him so that he could give him directions to a certain place he had to journey to.

After studying the map, the young man said, "If you continue on this path you will need to travel 5000 kms." the old man was aghast; "how long is the other route?" he asked.

"Only two kilometres," replied the boy.

Our journey through this lifetime can also be perceived as just 2kms when we use prayer and meditation to guide and help our Soul along its journey towards the Divine.

The more spiritually tuned-in we are the easier our journey back to the spiritual realm will be.

I hope this book will give you a better understanding of your spiritual nature and help you to develop it further.

How then do we grow, evolve, spiritually?

Our journey through this lifetime is often like travelling along a line.

My grandfather was literally travelling along a line, being a railway line at the time of one of his spiritual experiences.

Sometimes we might find ourselves being a leader, sometimes a follower.

It does not matter where we are in that line; whether in front or at the rear, what is important is the exact spot, circumstances we are in at that time as we can never have it back again.

Our position in that line is constantly teaching us the lessons life wants us to learn so that we may grow into the joyful souls we were sent here to be, totally in harmony with ourselves and one another.

But this harmony can only be achieved when we bring our body, mind, and soul into balance through our own enduring capacity, power and wisdom that come from external and internal knowledge. It is this wisdom that gives us power, which in turn gives us the capacity to endure the trials and tribulations of this lifetime here on earth.

When we pursue knowledge with enthusiasm and humility, we will acquire a vision of the Divine – our true Self. Then only after we have got it right within ourselves, can we achieve this harmony with others.

Ultimately, we are responsible for our own success or failure.

It is like playing a musical instrument – we need to first master it ourselves before we can play in an orchestra.

This little story depicts it well:

An old Japanese man went to live in the city with his son.

The first day he went for a walk and whilst walking he heard an unpleasant sound.

He saw a young boy playing the violin.

The old man decided that was the worst sounding instrument on earth and hurriedly walked on. The next day on his walk he went along another route, this time he heard a beautiful sound, almost like being in heaven he thought.

He came upon a woman, who was a maestro, and to his disbelief she was playing the same instrument, but this was totally different. He paused awhile to listen.

The following day his walk took him past a hall, this time he heard a sound that was truly exquisite, and it seemed to touch him deep down into his soul.

He approached the hall quietly, almost relevantly and looked inside. There he gazed upon an orchestra where each member was playing in total harmony with one another.

In awe he stood there and listened to them playing and once again thought this surely must be heaven.

When there is balance in our lives, we play our lives like a beautiful orchestra.

But finding this joy and peace during our earthly life is not easy.

We need guidance from our soul, our inner self, to be able to cope in whatever situation comes our way with confidence and love.

Some people follow a particular religious path in their quest to find this harmony and peace.

That is how it was for Grace Parker whose religion inspired her to do so much with her life.

She was born in Sydney, Australia in 1894 to Irish parents – the 13th child who was born, physically a very weak baby.

Her poems inspired many and one of them, 'Not Very strong' shows her inner strength triumphed over her physical weakness.

When I set out to earn my crust
board with strangers
take the ups and downs of life,
do the best I could,
I knew I was not very, strong -
it would not be easy, in the work force,
to survive in adulthood
religion was an enormous help,
as it should always be
to unlock our own reserves of power
it is our ever-present key.

She wrote her last book of poems Quiet Thoughts
at 93 years of age and lived to 107.

If you are following a particular religious path, then use your own judgement and wisdom to achieve this higher level of consciousness through your beliefs. Remember to dedicate yourself to your faith with humility, and never fall into the trap of belittling the faith of others while extolling your own. Even though we exist separately in reality we are all one.

If on the other hand you are seeking a particular religious faith then choose one that spreads love and compassion for all life on earth, and with guidance and purpose it will lead you to your higher Self. It is only through contemplation of the unseen that we can understand our divine nature.

A learned Guru, Hindu teacher, once said -
"A drop of water leaps in the air as long as it is just a drop.
It realizes what it really is only when it mingles with the sea."

And another learned Swami said -

"Religion is the eternal relation between the eternal soul and the eternal divine."

The great Indian leader Mahatma Gandhi said -

"Religion is not alien to us – it is always within us, for some consciously and for others unconsciously. But it is always there."

This brief description of the different religions might help you in your search for understanding of the beliefs and practices of some of the great faiths.

Hinduism is the worlds' oldest religion and has been in existence for over 5000 years.

Its stories were first passed on by word of mouth before being written in Sanskrit to form its sacred texts, the oldest and most sacred being the Rig Veda which contains over a thousand hymns.

It is practised all over the world, predominantly in India.

Hindus worship Brahman (God).

A Hindu story tells how a yogi, wise man, taught his son about Brahman by asking him to put some salt into water then to take it out again.

Of course, his son could not take it out.

The father told his son that Brahman is like the salt in the water-invisible but everywhere. Hindus believe that there are thousands of spirit guides helping mankind. These guides are not equal to Brahman but powerful spiritual beings like Saints, in Christianity.

They are referred to as Gods and Goddesses.

Sarasvati is the Goddess of wisdom and knowledge. Hindus believe that without knowledge one lives in darkness. They celebrate Diwali, the festival of lights.

They believe that the preservation of the world is our responsibility and have no 'rules as to how people should live their lives, believing that everyone will arrive at their destination at the correct time.

According to Hinduism people do not have just one lifetime here on Earth, but live in an endless cycle of life, death, and rebirth. This cycle is called Samsara and is seen as difficult, and at times pointless, which Hindus hope eventually to be freed from.

The symbol of a wheel, known as the Wheel of Life, stands for Samsara.

The Hindus have a lovely story about this wheel of life taking them on their journey through this lifetime.

The hub of the wheel, in the centre, holding the spokes and the wheel together is Brahman.

If that is strong the wheel will last through eternity.

Each spoke represents different nations of the world.

They are all the same because if one is lost the whole wheel weakens.

The rim represents the journey itself. Sometimes the wheel picks up 'shit' from the road, in some places in India, cows and other animals walk around freely. Hindus say not to get too concerned about this because it will soon dry and fall off.

Perhaps the journey requires the wheel to travel uphill. Hindus say that if feelings of doubt arise, I shall never make it, do not despair, if the hub is strong the wheel will reach the top.

On the other hand, travelling downhill can cause anxiety it is all happening too fast; Hindus say that instead of fearing the speed, enjoy it, and feel the joy of getting to one's destination sooner. Then there will be times when the wheel lands into a ditch.

In situations like these a person has three choices:

Stay there and allow it to become your journey's end. This choice is giving up in despair; Narayandutta Shrimali, a notable practitioner of Tantra Yoga says,

"Those who sit by the sea-shore get only the sea-shells. It is those who dive deep, who collect the pearls." When we are faced with failure or hardships we must not give up—we must move on. Life requires us to face up to our challenges. The quote, I have only failed if I have never tried, tells us that someone who could not take risks does not achieve anything. Courageous people move on and find they become richer in adversity and stronger in opposition. Shrimali says, "Only a coward is afraid of failure.

Even when alive he is like a dead man if he is afraid of death."

The second choice is to attempt to go it alone, by getting the wheel out of the ditch without any assistance. This is when the pride and ego, the negative aspects of our personality, come to the fore and stop us from reaching out. This is not the action for us to take because it will only make us feel physically, emotionally, mentally, and spiritually weaker because in most cases it is beyond the capacity of the average person to overcome a difficult situation alone.

Hindus believe that we must reach out for help—this is our third choice and the way to go. When we let go of all our pride and prejudices and in humility graciously accept assistance we can continue with our journey, on the right path again with a new confidence.

This act of receiving teaches us how to give in life.

A Hindu proverb says – those who give have all things. Those who withhold have nothing.

Hindus believe that our situation in this lifetime depends on Karma from the previous lifetime. Karma refers to the actions performed by an individual during a lifetime. A good action takes the person towards a better rebirth and eventually to Moksha, release from the cycle of rebirth. Someone can achieve Moksha only when they replace their ignorance with wisdom, the wisdom of the soul.

To help them develop their spirituality Hindus practise Meditation and Yoga.

There are four main types of Yoga:
Karma Yoga is the discipline of action.
Bhakti Yoga is the discipline of devotion.
Jnana Yoga is the discipline of knowledge.

Raja Yoga is the discipline of the mind through meditation.

To master the discipline of Yoga, Hindus use the energy from within, it is referred to in the Vedas as: All you are, and can ever be, is the energy available to you, on every level of your being. Hindu mystics call these energy centres Chakras this is a Sanskrit word meaning wheel that describes nerve clusters within the body that create vortices of energy. They tell us that when we activate this internal energy, we can follow our path in life with faith and confidence.

An explanation of the Chakras is given in Chapter Three of this book.

Buddhism on the other hand began some 3000 years ago.

Those who follow Buddhism follow the path of Buddha, their leader. He gave his followers the Eightfold Path which he said would give them eternal bliss, enlightenment.

Right view - point - right attitude to life.
Right values - consideration and compassion for others.

Right speech - avoid anger and gossip.

Right action's - living honestly and not harming others.

Right livelihood - avoiding jobs that harm anyone.

Right effort - think good thoughts.

Right mind - keeping the mind free from distraction.

Right meditations - leading to enlightenment.

Buddha taught his followers that life is suffering but if they embraced the Truth suffering would cease.

Their spiritual leader today is the Dalai Lama who lives in India.

Buddhists believe in reincarnation and that human beings have lived many, many lifetimes on Earth; each lifetime being to help individuals to evolve spiritually into enlightened beings so there would be no more lifetimes on Earth. Their focus is on devotion and deep meditation.

In Zen Buddhism devotees sit for long periods of time in the lotus position, and contemplate such thoughts as, life and death are in the mind, and nowhere else.

This extension of the mind helps them to embrace other profound avenues of thought which then breaks the chains of rigidity and frees the mind from sense perception alone.

This freedom allows them to exist in harmony with all living things so that when the breath has ceased, the knower will be experiencing the Clear Light of the natural condition,' from a Tibetan holy book.

Christians believe in Jesus Christ, who instructed them to follow The Ten Commandments and to love your neighbour, all people, as yourself.

Jesus taught his followers that the Kingdom of God was within, and that the Holy Spirit, the divine energy, would guide and sustain all people during their earthly life.

He told his followers to work for the spiritual welfare of all humankind through goodness and truth and he gave them eight universal truths to find happiness, which Christians know as The Sermon on the Mount.

Happy are those who know they are spiritually weak they will find the kingdom of God.

Happy are those who mourn, God will comfort them.

Happy are those who are humble, God will bless them.

Happy are those who do God's will, they shall have abundance.

Happy are those who show kindness to others, God will show them kindness.

Happy are those with a pure heart they shall see God.

Happy are those who work for peace, they belong to God.

Happy are those who persevere to do God's work, their reward is eternal Grace.

Christians believe that God has given them free will which is called Grace, to make their own choices; and that forgiveness, seeking forgiveness for themselves and forgiving others, will give them eternal blessings.

Christians believe in the Holy trinity, God the Father, God the Son and God the Holy Spirit which means God is part of everyone and everyone is part of God.

Their teachings are written in the Bible in two parts.

The Old Testament is about the covenant, promise, God made to his people through Abraham and Moses and the New Testament tells of the promise God made to his people through Jesus Christ. These Holy Scriptures teach Christians how to live a righteous life.

Jesus told his followers – I have come to give you abundance, which meant a complete joyful life on earth, and that even suffering can be changed into triumph.

For them the cross is a symbol of human suffering, whilst the resurrection represents the triumph of the spiritual body.

A pastor once referred to it as, turning your scars into stars.

Christians celebrate two important festivals in the year: the celebration of the birth of Jesus – Christmas; and Easter, when they remember his death and resurrection.

Christians believe that when they die their soul will return to Heaven, its original home of peacefulness.

Islam began some 500 years after Christianity.

Followers of Islam are called Muslims. They follow the teachings of the Prophet Muhammad. They follow a strict code of behaviour and worship Allah, God, and His Angels.

They believe that doing good deeds will get them into Paradise.

Muhammad taught them that the only way they will find peace is by doing the will of Allah.

Their Holy Book is the Koran. It teaches mercy, peace, justice, tolerance, and patience.

The Prophet Muhammad told his followers –

Do you know what is better than prayer, fasting and charity?

It is keeping good relations between people as quarrels and bad feelings destroy mankind.

They believe in Abraham, Moses, Noah, and Jesus.

Judaism began about 4000 years ago.

The Jews believe in God and like Christians follow the Ten Commandments.

They have known enormous suffering along their journey and were exiled from their lands many times, but their faith kept them strong.

Their belief is a reflection, of their own experiences of a living God in their earthly life.

It is enhanced through the words of the Shoah Liturgy – "I believe in the sun, even when it is not shining; I believe in love, even when feeling it not; I believe in God, even when God is silent." They believe they are God's chosen people, and trace their ancestry back to Abraham, and call themselves children of Abraham.

They have many Prophets who have led them on their journey to God.

Jews see God as the Creator and Ruler of all that is, all-powerful and all loving.

Their sacred writings are contained in the Tanakh. This contains histories, prophecies, poems, hymns, and sayings that were written down thousands of years ago.

Their symbol is the Star of David which represents light and wisdom to guide them on their journey. It is a symbol of leadership.

The holiest site for the Jews is 'The Wailing Wall' in Jerusalem. It is the remains of a temple built by King Herod 2000 years ago. Jewish people come from all over the world to pray at the wall. The Jews celebrate Hanukkah, the festival of Lights.

They believe that when they die their Soul will return to God where it originally came from.

The Bahais believe it is God's will that his followers should try and unite humanity by bringing all the faiths of the world together in harmony, and then there will be a new age of peace and justice and an end to all religious and racial prejudice.

Their faith began some 500 years ago from Islam, in the same way Christianity arose from Judaism. Their prophet is Baha'u'llah, which means Glory of God.

The symbol of Bahaism is a nine-pointed star.

Followers of Taoism practice a form of meditation based on a sequence of slow movements called Tai Chi. They believe this helps an individual's energy force to merge with the universal spiritual force. It is only through the merging of these forces that they will be able to live in harmony with themselves and others.

The religions of the indigenous people of America, and Australia, are linked with the Spirit world and deeply connected with the Earth.

Native American Indians followed the path of the Seven Sacred Rites to bring them into oneness with the Supernatural Power, the Great Spirit. They believed the natural and super-natural intertwined through meditation, chanting and dance, which they referred to as the Blessing Way. The great Apache leader Geronimo said he received his incredible Power from the Great Spirit these included visions of future events and voices instructing him what to do.

The brutal slaughter of his mother, wife and three children at their camp while Geronimo was in town getting supplies caused him such horror and pain it made him lose all sense of reality.

For days he wandered around aimlessly. Then one day, whilst in trance-like meditation, he heard his name called four times; four being an Apache sacred number, incidentally numerologists say that America is governed by the number four.

The message Geronimo received from the spirit world was that no bullet would ever kill him.

He believed this throughout his life and so did the other Apache's because even after being fired at many times no bullet ever killed him.

The Apache also believed that it was this power that enabled him to run 100 miles in a day and jog up mountains. When Geronimo finally surrendered in old age, he told General Crook,

"There is one God looking down on us all. We are all children of the one God. Once I moved about like the wind, now I surrender."

The close ties the American Indians had with their ancestral land compelled Geronimo to plead with the American Government to allow him to return to his homeland to die.

But this request was never granted. Today a stone eagle marks his grave.

Like the Hindus, the image of the Snake and the Wheel are sacred symbols to the American Indians as it depicts the journey of all creation.

The Australian Aborigines have a strong belief in their soul, self, that is one with the eternal Dreamtime.

Dreamtime is the beginning of life with no end.

They believe in a connection between their self and the guardian spirits of their ancestors.

An Elder told me that neither books nor intellectual knowledge was required for them to survive in spaces of emptiness. They could find a small water hole in a vast featureless plain through confidence in the ability of self, their inner guidance. Their ability to live in the harshness of the Australian outback was not instinctual as much as it was their connection to the land. The Elder told me it was this sensitivity to the Earth that allowed them to feel its vibrations.

Today many Aboriginal people believe that some of their people have lost their soul—like lost souls their life has no purpose; their connection with the earth has gone and they have forgotten, through lack of practice, how to go deep within to find their answers.

This brief account of some of the religions in the world today shows us that there really is not much difference in them, especially when you consider that all religions endeavour to show the way to spiritual fulfilment.

Dr. Arthur Peacocke, a notable Oxford Christian priest and biochemist and the winner of the Templeton Prize for Progress in Religion, gives some excellent guidance for seekers of a religious path.

'Religion must aim to depict reality and must be subject to continual critical scrutiny.'

He also says, "Religion is the pursuit of Truth and, at the end of the day, you cannot actually prove anything absolutely."

Dr. Peacocke states that we can find a pathway to God simply by reflecting on the natural world.

This is how guru Narayandutta experienced it, ""Today man has become artificial. He is deceitful, dishonest, and immoral. But he has not been able to detach himself from nature.

He builds huge houses then plants trees to beautify them because the very base of his life is nature. Distances from it makes a man superficial and hollow. I have lived all by myself in the jungles where the earth has been my bed and the sky my top sheet. I possessed nothing yet I considered myself the most fortunate person in the world as I had nature with me in its endless myriad of forms. I was fascinated with its changing face.

Closeness to nature has always given me happiness and contentment."

Religion is only good for the spiritual development of a person when it allows them to learn and grow at their own pace.

Secure, spiritually strong, religious leaders educate their followers while insecure, spiritually weak, leaders indoctrinate. Take a good look at the priest or guru or teacher before you allow yourself to be a participant of any faith.

Robine Courtin, a Buddhist nun says,

"Any religion that makes you a better person is the right one for you."

Scholars of theology have acknowledged three fatal flaws with many of today's religions.

They refer to them as the three great predicaments.

The 'egocentric' predicament is the limitations imposed by the self. For example, we can sympathize with another human being, but we can never see it exactly from their point of view because our experiences are different.

Native Americans say, "Walk a mile in my moccasins before you make a judgement on me."

The egocentric predicament, or illusion, leads us to make aristocratic claims about our faith—this is the belief that we are more blessed, special, than others in God's eyes and leads to the ethnocentric predicament which is the assumption that our religion is superior to any other.

Now let us put the above into a simple jingle—
My religion is better than yours, ha-dee-ha-dee-ha-ha.
My god is a King, yours does not exist, ha-dee-ha-dee-ha-ha,
I am going to Heaven, you are going to Hell, ha-dee-ha-dee-ha-ha.

When parents and teachers indoctrinate children, this is how they interpret it; and this is how it was for me as a six-year-old growing up in India until an incident concerning a friend of mine changed my way of thinking forever.

One of my friends was a Sikh girl called Rathan. Being a Christian I was not allowed to visit her in her home, and I could not invite her into my home.

Fortunately, we could enjoy each other's company at school.

My mother always told me Christians went to Heaven and everyone else went to Hell.

Where would Rathan go?

"To Hell," would be my mother's firm reply. I knew that was not right.

Nonetheless, I told Rathan one day where she was going when she died.

The following day Rathan said to me with a huge smile, "My mum said that I'm not going to Hell. She said that both of us are going to Heaven because we are both God's angels."

I knew this answer was correct because it gave me an indescribable feeling of joy.

All religious observances, all acts of worship, all methods of spiritual development aim to provide a channel of communication with the Divine Soul.

There is a universally present urge, whether consciously or unconsciously, within every one of us to establish contact with the Creator and this can be traced back to the very beginning of man's existence. There is no one path that leads to this experience and the unceasing warfare amongst different religious groups is very detrimental to the wellbeing of our planet.

When we all accept the fact that each one of us is rooted inextricably in the same soil that has been prepared and watered by the same Creator then only will our souls be liberated.

Saint Peter from the Christian faith said, "I truly, understand that God shows no partiality.

In every nation, whoever does what is right, is acceptable to Him."

In other words, our morals must be pure before we can move toward the Supreme Being.

And Mahatma Gandhi said, "Instead of everyone trying to convert others—why cannot Christians become better Christians, Muslims better Muslims and Hindus better Hindus?"

Instead of focusing our energy onto what other people are doing wrong let us use the same energy to get our own faith right. And let us pray for all people to find peace, purity, and enlightenment in whatever path they have chosen.

When the Soul is liberated through the overhauling and reshaping of the personality, we spiritually unfold like the butterflies' wings and then a higher form of vital energy will permeate the whole Personality.

Some gurus call this the metamorphism of the physical and mental structure of oneself.

This is when we become more spiritually minded and less materialistic minded.

We commence life with an awareness of this spiritual energy within us and it is often discernible in thought and action from an early age. I once heard a man say that his two-year-old son had so much energy in him he could supply power to a whole street of houses!

Not only does their spiritual power manifest itself in a physical way but many children display powers of clairvoyance, seeing the unseen, and clairaudience, hearing the silent voice.

My friend's three-year-old was close to his grandmother. One day, after she died, whilst watching TV she heard her son say, "Hello Grandma." When she asked her son "Who was there Paul?" he casually replied, "Oh, it was just Grandma saying hello."

And recently a relative of mine died and while I was sitting chatting to his three-year-old granddaughter she suddenly put her finger to her lips and said, "Shh granddad is here," and with a big smile on her face she kept looking towards the front door.

Never be concerned about your children's imaginary friends as they are most likely to be children in spirit, because their spiritual nature is still dominating their physical nature.

Keep it this way for as long as possible by teaching them gratitude and thankfulness for everything good that comes their way, because as they get older their humanness will become more dominant and their spiritual nature will slip further and further into the background. Though some may remain consciously aware of this gift throughout their lives and use it, others, due to the nature of the human mind, will dismiss it as weird or irrelevant. This is a dreadful misfortune because they can help others with this deeper insight just as my grandfather did. Some faiths believe that supernatural gifts are passed on to people by their ancestors.

Perhaps genetics play a part in these unusual gifts too.

A friend of mine has been endowed with the gift of seeing auras since he was a little boy but as he grew older his mind saw this extraordinary gift as freakish, abnormal, and it became an embarrassment to him. He saw this remarkable variation between himself and others as a negative trait and therefore never pursued it any further.

It would be the same for someone who is born a musician, but never uses this talent, because he is surrounded by people who consider playing a musical instrument, unproductive, or worse still, stupid.

It took my friend fifty years to tell me, only one of two people, what his inner mind could see.

It is amazing how people will openly give recognition to people who are physically, intellectually, or creatively talented, yet ridicule those who are spiritually talented.

Perhaps it is because the public, at large, is ignorant to the fact that there exists a basic and fundamental difference in spiritual consciousness. My grandfather, for example, was obviously a man at a higher spiritual consciousness level than his fireman.

The evolution of man signifies the evolution of his consciousness to the super conscious level.

If we go back to the earliest civilizations in India, Egypt or China, this super-sensory wisdom was given even more recognition to the people who were endowed with it than what we give to our sporting heroes or musicians today.

All ancient religious texts have stories of these gifted people on earth communicating with the spiritual realm. Whether it was through messages, visions, dreams, or signs this connection to the divine was clearly and openly expressed and acknowledged.

One of my favourite stories from the Bible is the Story of Joseph, a young man who used his super conscious mind to understand and interpret visions from dreams.

A long, long time ago in the land of Canaan there lived a young boy named Joseph.

He lived in a tent with his mother and father and ten brothers.

Every morning his older brothers took the sheep out of their pens to graze beyond the nearby hills and every evening they returned to their tent before dusk.

Joseph loved to hear their stories of how they fought mountain lions or wolves that were trying to steal their sheep, and every day he would longingly ask his father if he could join his brothers. But each day the answer was the same, "Not till you are older Joseph."

One day, perhaps it was to cheer Joseph up, his father Jacob, told Joseph, "Today I will make you a new coat, with colours in it." Joseph was so excited.

All morning he busied himself collecting different coloured berries from the plants and bushes nearby, and with great interest he watched Jacob make the colours and then dye the cloth his mother had woven.

When the coat was ready, he put it on—it felt so good.

He could not wait to show it to his brothers.

But when they came home, they took one look at him and laughed.

"A coat of many colours; how ridiculous! To hide his hurt Joseph laughed too, but from that moment on the joy of his new coat was lost forever.

Joseph continued to ask daily if he could accompany his brothers when they took the sheep to pasture, but his father's answer was always the same, "not yet."

Then, one day, to his delight his mother said he could go later in the day to his brothers and give them their mid-day meal, a heavy bean broth with some flat bread.

When the sun was directly overhead Joseph took the basket of food and set off.

He raced up the first little hill, but he could not see them; he scooted up the next hill, and there in the distance, he saw them with the sheep nearby. He waved excitedly to them, but no one waved back. Well, he was a fair way off so perhaps they had not spotted him yet.

He raced on until, breathless, he reached them and with a cheery grin he said,

"I've brought your meal." One of the brothers walked over to Joseph and grabbed him with such force it alarmed him, and he dropped the basket. Then another brother grabbed him by the throat. Surprise changed to fear for Joseph. He realized something was very wrong. Perhaps it was the coat? His mind was totally confused.

Then he heard one brother say, "Let's kill him."

"Why?" asked Joseph," because our father gives you everything and we are ignored, we hate you," was their reply. Joseph quickly said, "It is this coat, well, I don't like it either it is an awful coat; now I better get back to our tent otherwise our parents will be worried, and I promise I won't say anything." But his brothers would not release him.

Perhaps it was that dream—in which all his brothers were bowing down to him?

Why had he been silly enough to tell them about it?

But they had laughed at his 'stupid' dream they had not been angry.

His mind was totally confused.

The brothers tightened their hold on him and pulled off his coat,

Joseph looked from one to the other their eyes looked so angry.

Then Ruben, the eldest brother said, "Let's not kill him, let us throw him into the well instead."

Now fear totally overtook Joseph's senses. "No, not the well, please do not put me in the well," was his desperate plea.

For Joseph, any fate was better than being thrown into that old abandoned well, wasn't it filled with snakes, spiders, and other creepy insects?

Then all he could hear was the echo of his screams as he felt himself falling down the well.

He landed on something soft. How cold and dark it was down there.

His father had told him that if you stay very still snakes will not harm you. Many thoughts began to crowd his mind. After some moments, his eyes adjusted to the darkness. There did not appear to be anything alive down there, just a few bones so perhaps a sheep had fallen in many years ago.

He looked up, there was light up above. His thoughts were racing in his head.

'When the boys return home without me my father will come looking for me. He's sure to look in this well then I'll scream out loudly and he'll rescue me.'

So, Joseph fixed his gaze to the top of the well and lost all sense of time.

Suddenly he heard voices, "My brothers have come back for me," he thought. Relief filled every bone in his body. Then he heard Ruben call out, "Joseph catch this rope and we'll pull you out." He grabbed the rope with both hands and ran up the sides of the well.

There he saw his brothers standing around the well and Joseph said excitedly "I knew you were only teasing me; I promise I won't say anything about this to our parents."

But then he looked around and he saw that three strangers were talking to Ruben and Joseph began to scream like he had never screamed before.

"No Ruben, put me back into the well, please don't sell me. Our parents promised they would never sell any of us as slaves."

The three strangers approached him and took him firmly by the hand and led him away to where their camels were waiting. Joseph was tied onto a camel and slowly his journey into the unknown began.

With tears in his eyes, he looked at his homeland knowing he would never see it again.

At dusk, the brothers returned to their tent with their sheep.

When Jacob saw them coming, he anxiously raced out to meet them, "Where's Joseph?" he asked breathlessly.

"We haven't seen him father!" they replied.

Jacob said, "He left when the sun was overhead with your meal."

"We have had no meal today, Father," said Ruben, then, in a quiet voice, he said, "but we found this on our journey home." And he held up the torn bloodied coat of Joseph's.

Jacob broke down and wept and it was not long after that fateful day that Joseph's mother died from a broken heart.

Meanwhile Joseph and his captors, after riding for many days and nights, finally arrived at a large town. The language the people spoke and the way they dressed was very foreign to him.

In silence he had accepted his fate. He was taken to the market-place and there placed on a platform with other, younger, and older boys for sale.

Totally emotionless Joseph looked at the large crowd of people milling around.

Then he looked into the eyes of a man he had never seen before, but felt he knew.

In humbleness Joseph lowered his gaze to the ground and when he looked up again, the man was gone.

A short while later the bidding started.

Joseph realized they were bidding for him, and he felt a surge of joy go through him when the man he had noticed earlier came up to the platform and led him away.

Joseph made a promise to himself, there and then, that he would be the best slave any master could ever wish for.

He learnt fast and his master often told him that purchasing him was the best thing he had ever done. His master often wondered why Joseph's parents had sold him and who they were. However, those were questions Joseph never wished to answer. He was happy now and memories of the past only made him sad.

The years passed, and then one day his master came home deeply concerned.

As an adviser to the Pharaoh, he had to have an answer to all the Pharaohs questions and now the Pharaoh had given him a question he was unable to answer, that concerned the Pharaohs dream. Joseph implored his master "Please take me to the Pharaoh because I can interpret dreams, I've had this gift all my life master." So reluctantly his master agreed to take Joseph to see the Pharaoh, knowing that an incorrect interpretation of the dream could result in both their deaths.

The splendour of the Pharaohs palace took Joseph's breath away; the beautiful white and black marble, the water fountains, the elaborate silken rugs, and the golden ornaments were to a slave's eyes almost unbelievable.

He humbly bowed before the Pharaoh and earnestly listened to his dream.

What an amazing dream thought Joseph. Seven fat cows grazing contentedly in a lush green meadow when suddenly, over the hill, appears seven very lean cows who immediately devour the seven fat cows.

Joseph stayed silent for a few moments and then in a voice of authority spoke.

"The seven fat cows, your majesty, represent seven years of plenty in your land.

This is when there will be plenty of rain, the crops will grow, the fruit trees will yield a large amount of fruit, the grass will be lush, and your people and your animals will live in a land of plenty.

The eighth year will mark the beginning of a dreadful drought. The likes of which have never been seen in this land before. For seven years there will be no rain, the grass will dry up then the trees will die. Slowly your animals will start to die then your people."

The Pharaoh said, "You are a man of great wisdom slave. No one in my kingdom has been able to interpret my dream except you so tell me, wise slave, what can be done to avoid the deaths of my people and my animals?"

Joseph put forward a plan to the Pharaoh to build storage sheds and barns to store the grain during the years of plenty.

Then Pharaoh made Joseph Governor of all of Egypt. He gave him a palace to live in with untold wealth at his disposal and Joseph married a Princess.

And so it was, after the seven years of plenty the land was indeed in the grips of drought.

People came from far and wide to buy food because there was no food in any of the neighbouring lands.

Meanwhile, back in the land of Canaan Jacob was now an old man and almost blind.

He was deeply concerned about the drought that was causing his sheep to die daily. The older brothers wanted to go to this far away land and purchase food, but Jacob wondered whether he should let them go. What if they did not return like his other son Joseph?

The years had not lessened the pain in his heart from losing Joseph.

Finally, Jacob agreed to let four of his sons go. He gave them the few gold coins he had to purchase food then he watched them leave with a heavy heart.

It so happened that the day the brothers arrived in Egypt to buy the food Joseph was doing one of his many inspection rounds of the long queues of people waiting to buy food.

He stopped his chariot near four foreigners and was amazed that he understood the language they were speaking. 'It couldn't be, he thought?'

His heart was beating quickly.

He got one of his men to go to them and ask them what their names were and from which land they had come? When the man told Joseph their names and that they were from the land of Canaan Joseph felt a sharp pain go through his heart,

"They are my brothers", he whispered to himself.

He moved quickly to the top of the queue and called the food-distributor to one side and instructed him to "give the four foreigners in the queue whatever food they required and then place their money back into the food bag before handing it over to them."

So, when it was their turn, the brothers paid for their food and were on their way home when suddenly they heard horses approaching.

In a loud voice someone commanded them to stop. "Who was this man, was he the Pharaoh?" they wondered. He ordered their bags to be searched and the guards found gold coins amongst the grain.

The brothers were astonished, they begged for mercy saying they had no idea how the money got there.

They had not the slightest notion that this Pharaoh was their brother Joseph.

After all he had been just a skinny lad when they sold him, now he was a man of strength and wealth, with all the majesty of an Egyptian Pharaoh.

Without giving the brothers a hint of his identity, Joseph commanded them to return to Canaan and bring the rest of their family back to Egypt.

To make sure they honoured his command he told them that two of the brothers would be taken as prisoners until the others returned and if they did not return within the month the two brothers would be killed.

Each day passed with painful slowness for Joseph.

There were days when he bitterly regretted what he had done because he knew that if his family did not return to Egypt, he would have to have his brothers killed because, as the Governor of Egypt, if he decreed something it had to be carried through.

And then one day, on his many rides to the outskirts of the town he saw his brothers coming. He could hardly believe what he was seeing.

He raced in his chariot towards them but stopped a few paces in front.

Then he walked towards them. The brothers stopped and bowed low; but old Jacob walked on, slowly, and hesitantly.

Gradually through his blurred vision he began to see a large man in front of him.

Then he said, "Joseph, is it you Joseph?"

And Joseph walked into his father's outstretched arms.

The brothers looked on shocked and speechless.

Joseph however never told his father the true succession of events as he felt that it would change nothing, and it was so wonderful to be with them all again.

From that day on they lived together in Egypt.

In this story Joseph receives his visions in dreams. The brothers bowing down to him for example, and he also has the gift of interpreting dreams.

Another Joseph in the Bible, Mary's husband, also received messages from the spirit realm in his dreams. His marriage to Mary and the birth of Jesus was told' to him in a dream before any verbal message was given to him.

For Christians, the birth of Jesus is filled with supernatural occurrences—ordinary shepherds see a brilliant light and hear voices, three wise men, possibly astronomers, see and follow a bright star to the place of Jesus' birth.

These events were of such astounding significance they were recorded and have been believed for thousands of years.

And that is how it is with all the religious faiths, the recorded occurrences of supernatural events which believers have believed and respected from the time of their recording to this present day.

And it is not just people from religious history who had these experiences.

Abraham Lincoln was warned of his assassination in a dream but chose to ignore it.

In contrast, Napoleon Bonaparte used messages from his dreams in the planning of his military victories.

James Watt, one of the inventors of the steam engine, developed ball bearings thanks to a persistent series of recurring dreams.

These stories were told by these people themselves and were later included in their biographies. And just as people have doubts and want proof of these supernatural happenings today, thousands of years ago there were also the unbelievers and the sceptics.

Today our advanced technology is helping to clarify many of the hitherto invisible properties of the spiritual realm. An example of this is aura photography.

Whilst scientists are rewriting more and more of the facts of the past, many unbelievable stories of the past are becoming factual today.

The latest medical research, conducted by a team of Dutch doctors, supports the view that even after death there is still life being recorded on monitors.

Is it the Soul? Is the mind still active?

Scientists, too, are pushing ahead with further research into this 'super organic psychic phenomena' of a spiritual soul.

Whatever your beliefs remember to be open minded on all topics because it is only through the expansion of the mind that we can grow in wisdom.

When we find time during our busy waking hours to still the mind, as in deep meditation, it is easier to become aware of this inner wisdom.

Our dreams too can become a form of spiritual guidance along with the practice of meditation because it is only when we still the mind that the super conscious mind can emerge.

If using people of psychic ability, to obtain messages for yourself, remember to get your own answers from deep within.

Choose what is relevant and useful and discard whatever messages you feel uncomfortable with. After all, just as there are many excellent clairvoyants, psychics, and the like around, there are many that do not receive messages clearly or cannot interrupt them accurately.

This happens when the conscious mind becomes active before a 'reading' is completed.

You will find, however, that with regular meditation you will receive your own answers for your life and the need to go elsewhere will diminish.

Try to become aware of every aspect of your life even while you are in a dream state.

Keep a note pad beside your bed and write down whatever you remember of a dream immediately upon awakening.

Be aware of how you feel during your everyday activities, a diary helps here, because the more you get to know yourself the more comfortable you will become with yourself which in turn will lead to a feeling of contentment.

You must know yourself first before you can get to know and understand others.

This is the most essential prerequisite for having a successful relationship with someone else because the more you understand yourself the better you will understand others.

Knowledge in the spirit of open inquiry, remember nothing is simply black or white, gives us the wisdom and insight to properly, consider our feelings.

It allows us to view life's questions with an open mind and this enables us to live amicably with our fellow human beings.

Winston Churchill said, "The empires of the future are the empires of the mind."

Today, most people will acknowledge that it is through the power of the mind that we find success and happiness. However, what many people are not aware of is that this power can be enhanced when we tap into our super-consciousness mind.

This is achieved through the practice of meditation and the release of the energy from within.

Our genetic make-up will dictate whether we have an ear for music are good at sport or how attractive we appear to the opposite sex. When we combine these endowments with inner wisdom and vitality there is an overall improvement.

For example, if a musically talented person becomes divinely inspired this higher level of consciousness will take their musical ability to its highest potential because it becomes an expression of the body, mind, and soul.

It is the same for natural beauty. We know that it can be improved with correct diet and exercise and fashion, but when the spiritual energy is used a glow will be added to one's appearance, an inner radiance and then the already beautiful person become even more beautiful.

For older people, the practice of meditation and yoga can slow down the aging process because this vital inner energy restores damaged and diseased cells within the body.

Whilst some people are smarter, some more attractive, and some more athletic than others, everyone has the same level of spiritual energy within.

Everyone is connected to the same divine source, universal energy, so not to use this power makes no sense at all. However, because it cannot be explained rationally some people dismiss it as meaningless and unreal, even though deep down they feel unsure.

In the movie 'Strictly Ballroom' there is a scene in which an older lady is trying to get the main actor to dance with more meaning. He has been to dancing school, and he knows all the correct steps yet there is something missing in his dancing. The woman touches his chest and says, "Dancing is not dancing unless it comes from within."

She wanted more spiritual energy in his dancing, not just the physical energy.

As more and more people begin using this extra power in their own personal experiences its understanding will become more widely acknowledged. When we put our body, mind, and soul into everything we do, our energy is strengthened by the vital currents of the divine cosmic energy and then our **ach**ievements become amazing.

But to make this energy work to our benefit we need to reach out and use it to help make this world of ours a better place for everyone.

The more we use this energy for the good of all, the more energy we will generate for ourselves because its source is eternal.

Recently, an anonymous Irish inventor claimed that he could create free energy.

We certainly can when we use the spiritual energy from within.

Today, many people are using this inner energy to work for the preservation of our planet and in many countries, Governments have listened to the voices of the people. As a result, our whales, our rain forests, and even our sand dunes have become protected. These people work diligently, with certainty and purpose, to correct the injustices they see around them.

Like Fran Peavey, an American activist who was a strong voice for the anti-apartheid movement in South Africa. She also worked tirelessly to stop the pollution in the rivers of India, which led to a greater awareness of the plight of the few remaining fresh-water dolphins in the world.

These dolphins are small and blind, probably due to the polluted rivers. Because of Fran Peaveys work the dolphins might survive.

She worked passionately with the rape victims of war-torn Yugoslavia, even putting her own life at risk on occasions, and has been a forceful voice against nuclear weapons both in her own country and abroad.

Fran believes that our purpose for being here is to help one another because, she says, "We are all connected to each another."

She uses the analogy of crabgrass to define this. Each blade appears to be growing on its own; but if you try to pull up one blade of grass you will find that all the blades of grass are connected to the same root system.

What is the secret of her success with so many varied projects?

Fran uses two words, listening and reflection.

When we reflect on what we have heard or seen we are meditating on it, and it is through meditation that we can tap into our super conscious mind from where we get a clear understanding of our purpose for being here.

It is this deep reflection that gives us the guidelines to take whatever action is necessary for us to lead successful and fulfilling lives.

Chapter Two

TUNING-IN THROUGH THE EARS/YEARS. LISTENING-IN INTUITIVELY

Most people today do not possess adequate listening skills and that is why there are so many relationship problems within the family and work force.

There is only one correct form of listening when communicating with each other and that is via the soul.

Our ears are the physical aspect of listening, that transmits information to the brain for logical interpretation, but when we listen through the Soul, we get a more intelligent and truthful interpretation, this form of listening shows the highest level of respect for another person and towards oneself.

It is not possible for all of us to be involved in projects of the same magnitude as those Fran Peavey gets involved with, but we can all try to perfect our listening skills and that alone will make a difference to our world.

When we acquire this truly divine gift, the art of listening from the soul, every aspect of our lives will improve.

We will become better parents, better employers, better friends, and better teammates.

And because we are all inter-connected when we improve everybody else does too.

Most parents love and nurture their children unselfishly they cater for all their physical needs; they support them emotionally and spend large sums of money and time on their education and learning programs. Many parents guide them in their spiritual development but very few help their children to listen to their inner voice.

This is the key to having responsible, well-adjusted children.

Later in my book I will give some simple meditation exercises for children that will develop these listening skills.

Usually when children do not listen it is because parents and adults do not listen.

This is so evident in cases of sexual abuse.

A young girl came to me once very distraught and suicidal. An older brother had sexually abused her since the age of nine and then in her teenage years she felt the need to tell her mother, but her mother refused to believe her.

For the mother, the truth was too painful so, using the logical side of her brain she set out to prove the allegations were all lies.

She was a good mother so how could she have not known that this was occurring right in her own home?

Her son was a wonderful boy. He had always taken care of them while their father was away. The daughter on the other hand was spoilt and liked attention.

Maybe this was a new way of getting it?

She had started drinking heavily and hanging out with the wrong people.

All these thoughts were helping to convince the mother that her son could never have committed such a despicable act.

This is what the mother's conscious mind, wanted to believe and listen to.

She did not want to hear and believe the pain and shame of her daughter's abuse.

The Catholic Church's confessional booth has been the brunt of many a joke over the years but the concept, is a good one because it gives people an opportunity to be listened to.

The benefits are two-fold; the "confessor' has an opportunity to release concerns they have within them and in turn it gives them an opportunity to listen to advice or words of comfort from the priest. When it comes from within the results are only positive.

When we listen from deep within, we learn to differentiate between the truth and lies.

At some time in our lives many of us have been told:
"You're the only one for me",
"One day we'll get married." "I'll do anything for you."
"Come and see me and I'll give you the job you're looking for."

We listen to all this, and our conscious mind will interpret it in exactly the way we have conditioned it to do. If we are doubters, we will consider it as being all lies even if it is the truth. Because that is the way the mind wants to go.

"You've heard this before." "He/she doesn't mean it." "I'll believe it when I see it."

On the other hand, if we are believers because we assume people are truthful like ourselves, we will believe every word that is spoken.

Or perhaps our self-esteem needs a boost, so the mind jumps in and says,

"This is good believe it", and if we have never experienced dishonesty before it will then be natural for the mind to believe whatever a person says.

It is essential to learn, and to teach our children how to listen to that inner voice.

Only then will everyone get a truthful interpretation of the spoken word and they will receive guidance, to take the best action necessary.

With regular practice of meditation and reflection our blind ignorance will change to a new intelligent awareness, that will enable us to make choices and decisions that will enrich our lives.

Knowledge helps us to find possibilities where once we saw problems.

When we acquire true knowledge, we overcome fear.

For Hindus, the Lotus flower is the symbol of true knowledge and to gaze upon it whilst meditating will bring the truth into one's mind.

When we listen from within fear is released and the truth is revealed.

I call it the b and d of good listening skills.

What we listen to and believe and what we listen to and disbelieve or dismiss.

From a young age I remember my mother being constantly ill. I listened to each ailment which, my mother always told me was going to lead to her imminent death. The heavy cold was sure to develop into pneumonia. The dreadful swelling in her ankles must mean her body was filling up with fluid which caused death to come quickly, the pain in her chest meant she was on the verge of having a heart attack, and the persistent headache must mean she had a tumour on the brain.

I would sit on my bed imagining life with no mother, what would happen to me and my brothers and sisters? Because I had also listened to our mother telling us that our father would be incapable of caring adequately for us, so our fate was either a boarding school or worse still an orphanage. The more I listened, the more anxious and unhappy I became.

Then one day, while my mother was telling me about her newest ailment something from deep within me told me not to 'listen' anymore, and I literally turned a deaf ear to my mother's death causing illnesses.

From that moment on I was released from having to comprehend information that was far too difficult and painful for my young shoulders to carry.

Today my mother, who is well into her eighties, lives an independent and fairly, active life.

I listened but I disbelieved, and my mind gained peace.

This true story is about a young girl who listened and believed, and it literally saved her life.

The year was 1920. Alice was a happy nine-year-old living in Burma with her family.

She lived in a beautiful home with lots of pets.

Alice loved animals and birds and she enjoyed school and spending time with her friends.

And then one day Alice's whole life changed.

War broke out in Burma and people were being killed indiscriminately.

Houses were being looted and burnt. No one felt safe, not even in their own homes.

People started fleeing the country taking a few precious belongings with them. They had to walk because the soldiers had confiscated all types of transport.

Suddenly the war was taking place in Alice's once quiet leafy green street.

"We have to leave immediately," Alice's father said.

"But what about my pets?" asked Alice, "We'll come back for them," he said and then Alice's father knelt in front of her and looked into her eyes and said,

"Alice, promise me you will never look back."

The request bewildered her.

"Promise me Alice you will never look back until you see the Red Cross."

And Alice, with all her heart promised and then they were on their way. Walking and sometimes running in the same direction as everyone else was going. Some were moving along in shocked silence while others were shouting hysterically.

Alice held onto her father's hand with her mother and brothers nearby.

To Alice it seemed like a huge sea of people all going in the same direction.

There was a lot of bumping and pushing and Alice found herself running with the crowd, but she was not holding her father's hand.

Where was her father? where was her family? She instinctively wanted to look behind her but then she remembered her promise.

So instead of looking behind she looked ahead with her mind telling her that her family must be up ahead and that she must have got accidentally left behind amongst the frenzied crowds.

So, with her eyes looking forward she moved on hurriedly and then after what seemed like countless hours, she saw the Red Cross at the Indian border and she collapsed into the arms of a lady in a white dress.

Alice retained vivid memories of this lady in a white dress who was a nurse and became a nurse herself.

None of her family made that fateful journey.

Somewhere in that mad exodus they had all been killed.

Years later Alice was to marvel at her father's words of wisdom.

If she had looked back, she would have instinctively headed in that direction to search for her family but by keeping her eyes forward her focus was on moving ahead and it was that that saved her life.

When listening causes one to feel apprehension or fear it is a warning from the inner voice.

Some years ago, I was enjoying a quiet evening at home when there was a knock at my front door. I walked up to the door and called out, "Who is it?" and a young voice answered,

"Can you help me?"

Any adult, me included, would immediately have opened the door to find out what was wrong when it was a child calling for help. But at this time, I behaved in a most unusual fashion. Upon hearing the voice, I froze, and it took a few seconds before I could open the door.

Outside stood a young boy and as he looked at me fear went right through my body.

He said his family had just moved into the house behind us and that his mother wanted to borrow some cigarettes. I had difficulty telling him that I was 'sorry but no one smoked in my house. Then I shut the door and securely locked it. I stood there for a while feeling very disturbed. Afterwards I was quite annoyed with myself for feeling so scared because a child had knocked on my door.

The next evening there was another knock on my door, this time a lot louder and an adult's voice said, "Police."

I opened the door immediately.

The police told me that they were looking for little Karen from across the road. She had been playing near the creek bed earlier in the evening with my younger son and a few other children and had not returned home. They wanted to know whether I had seen her.

After door knocking at all the houses in the area the police brought in the rescue dogs and a search was organized. Everyone in the street got their flashlights and joined in the search for six-year-old Karen who was very tiny for her age.

We spent most of the night searching the bush land along the creek bed, then just before dawn Karen's little body was found.

She had been brutally bashed with a large rock and then hung from a low branch of a tree.

The boy who had knocked on my door the night before confessed to her murder.

The fear I had felt when I heard his voice had come from deep within me.

It had been a spiritual warning.

So often we go through life wishing we had listened to our parents, or teachers, or whoever gave us good advice at the time, which we ignored only to regret not listening when something went wrong.

On quite a few occasions I have said, "If I had listened to Mother this would not have happened." I heard her obviously because I could re-call the incident years later, but I had not listened wisely. When we listen from within, we accept the good advice and use it and then discard or disbelieve the rubbish.

The American President George Bush said on national television,

"I should have listened to you Mother when you told me to chew pretzels before swallowing them", after he had had a nasty choking experience which resulted in him being hospitalized.

The key to unlocking the door to our soul is through listening.

First, we must master the art of listening with our physical ears before we can reach that higher level of consciousness that will enable us to listen through super sensory perception.

To develop these powers, we need to begin with the first of our conscious senses which is that of hearing because this is our first and earliest connection to the natural world from the spiritual world.

The greatest discovery in human biology has been how the human ear evolved from its lower form to its development in the human embryo.

Practitioners of acupuncture link the ear to an inverted foetus and have identified over 120 pressure points in the ear as having a reflex response to other parts of the body.

Some 260,000,000 years ago certain fishes our ancestors, because all life on earth is inter-related through the same divine source, left the oceans to live on dry land and their discarded gills were transformed into the outer and middle ear.

This is one of the most remarkable adaptations of the entire process of evolution.

The earliest formation of the human ear begins before the embryo is three weeks old.

Babies are listening to sounds and voices in the womb.

Upon death the last thing to be extinguished is the ability to listen.

This sense perception is the first and last connection we have as a human being that is why it is the most important of all our senses.

Before we can see, or taste, or touch, or smell, and certainly before we can speak or read, we can listen.

Apart from the deaf everyone else learns everything in life through listening.

And not only is the ear responsible for hearing it also gives us balance (equilibrium).

And just as our hearing gives us physical balance, listening via the soul brings our body, mind, and soul into balance.

This sense of equilibrium is especially necessary in the dark when the eyes cannot help to maintain balance.

This can be looked at in the same way as Christians believe that the stronger the light of Christ within them the greater their balance or guidance when they are in darkness or adversity. Equilibrium developed long before hearing, in the process of evolution.

For animals, the sense of balance and hearing is vital for their survival because it gives them the instinctive response of the 'fight or flight' action.

This sense of hearing is very developed in cats, and they have excellent balance.

Does this heightened level of hearing make them intuitive?

Helen Keller, who was blind and deaf, wrote:

"The problems of deafness are deeper and more complex, if not more important than those of blindness. Deafness is a much worse misfortune, for it means the loss of the most vital stimulus, the sound of the voice, that brings language, sets thoughts astir and keeps us in the intellectual company of man."

Before her second birthday Helen was stricken with an illness that left her deaf and blind, and shortly afterwards she lost her speech also.

A remarkable teacher called Miss Sullivan taught Helen to read by placing shapes of the alphabet into her hand, and then she learnt to read and write in Braille.

Later, through her inner listening she wrote numerous books.

Beethoven too composed some of his finest music particularly his Adagio from the Moonlight Sonata when he was almost totally deaf.

His music was regarded as the most romantic of its time because it was infused with so much emotion.

One must wonder at the extraordinary achievements of these people, which defies explanation from a strictly rational mind.

How did they, with their obvious handicaps accomplish the impossible?

The only conceivable explanation would have to be that their inspiration and guidance came from internal sources rather than through hearing.

What their ears were unable to achieve they received through inner listening.

Yogis practice certain yoga postures to improve the blood flow to the inner ear and cochlea and they use the energy from the chakras to re-grow dead and damaged cells of the hearing nerves. At some Ashrams, Yoga and Meditation learning centres, Yogis will give their students certain tasks to perform to see whether they have reached a higher level of consciousness through their practice and the unblocking of their chakras.

One of the more common exercises are,

"Choose an unsuspecting person and ask them to sit in front of you.

Chant a mantra then ask the person to fetch you a glass of water through your mind.

Do this by looking into their eyes whilst thinking about the words.

If the person immediately gets up and performs the task you had in mind you know that you are using your inner voice successfully and the participant is doing the same through their inner listening."

Their aim is to move away from just using their physical senses to using their super-sensory powers which they believe is a gift of the spirit.

These acts of following non-verbal instructions, is evidence of a deeper level of human intelligence.

The main object of these yoga exercises is to take the conscious mind beyond the boundaries that confine the normal senses into the super-sensory regions of spiritual listening and to manifest a heightened level of equilibrium to create spiritual balance.

We know that our physical ears work through sound waves that cause the eardrum to vibrate.

In the same way chanting in meditation causes vibrations within our spiritual energy centres which then allows us to perceive things through inner listening when we become tuned-in to spiritual vibrations.

Buddhist monks and Indian yogis have a long tradition of chanting mantras and hymns for spiritual balance and cleansing.

The master Jesus often told his followers, "If any man has ears to hear let him hear."

He was referring to spiritual hearing that which we hear on a deeper level.

Once when a young boy was brought to Jesus to be healed because he suffered from convulsions that caused him to fall over Jesus addressed the illness as an 'unclean spirit.'

He said, "You dumb and deaf spirit, come out of him." And immediately the boy was healed.

Jesus knew that in to heal the boy completely he had to free the spiritual energy from within. In other words, the boy was made whole again both physically and spiritually.

Most people have heard about Morse code. A code used for transmitting messages through dots and dashes or by shorter and longer sounds.

Well, many years ago back when the telegraph was the fastest means of long-distance communication, there was a young man who applied for a job as a Morse code operator. Answering an advertisement in the newspaper, he went to the address that was listed in the advertisement.

When he arrived, he entered a large noisy office. In the background a telegraph clacked away.

A sign on the receptionist's counter instructed job applicants to fill out a form and wait until they were summoned to enter the inner office.

The young man completed his form and sat down with seven other waiting applicants.

After a few minutes, the young man stood up and crossed the room to the door of the inner office then walked in. The other applicants perked up wondering what was going on.

Why had this young man been so bold?

They muttered amongst themselves that they had not heard any summons to enter the office for an interview, and they took more than a little satisfaction in assuming the young man who went into the office would be reprimanded for his presumption and immediately disqualified for the job.

Within a few minutes he emerged from the inner office escorted by the interviewer who announced to the other applicants,

"Gentlemen, thank you very much for coming but the job has been filled by this young man."

The other applicants began grumbling to each other, and then one spoke up,

"Wait a minute. I do not understand. He was the last one to come in and we never even got a chance to be interviewed. Yet he got the job? That's not fair."

The employer responded: "All the time you've been sitting here the telegraph has been ticking out this message in Morse code,

'If you understand this message then come right in. The job is yours.

None of you heard it or understood it. This man did so the job is his."

The young man's keenness to get the job caused all his thoughts to be directed towards that goal and with concentrated listening, plus his ability to decipher the code made him the successful candidate.

Our lives too will be successful if we concentrate while listening.

A lot of people listen as if they are suffering from "jet-lag." They can only be focused for a few seconds before the mind wanders off again.

When we master the art of physical listening we will automatically learn to listen on a much deeper level.

Having the television constantly on or even the radio is a deterrent for internal listening because this external bombardment of noise damages the sensitive inner ear.

Some people use the noise to block out their thoughts – in other words instead of addressing problematic issues and getting solutions from within they try to use noise to chase them away. Unfortunately, they do not go away but stay lurking in the background waiting to be dealt with at another time.

Quiet, contemplative thoughts will help to solve all problems.

Tao teaching says that things are easier to control while things are quiet.

Amongst the tribal people talking circles were opportunities for issues to be dealt with quietly. The little bit of talking was done respectively and softly.

The silence from the listeners allowed the people to really contemplate the issues.

Today adults and children seem to be so loud and intense with their verbal interaction, one could even call it verbal hyperactivity.

No one wants to listen, and our numbers of children diagnosed with attention deficit disorders are increasing.

Inner listening gives us a heightened awareness of each situation which allows our perception to be more accurate and truthful.

The more we listen, the more peaceful we will become which leads to a healthier body and mind.

We use the right side of our brain for listening, while verbal expression is a function of the left brain. The more we listen the more we activate the right side of our brain.

Listening to different types of music, being aware of our dreams and using our imagination takes us to a higher level of consciousness.

Psychologists now believe that by enhancing the right side of the brain, listening side, we are less aggressive and feel more in control of our lives, this develops feelings of contentment and leads to good self-esteem.

Listening takes us into the next dimension of our Self. We become intuitive, we believe the Truth and we know the outcome before the experience, unlike hindsight!

The energy that permeates our whole being when we consciously strive to listen intuitively allows us to be extraordinary people. As adults reach this higher level of awareness, they can lead children to a higher level of consciousness too.

The greatest act of love that parents can bestow upon their offspring is to lovingly guide them towards developing their soul through super-sensory perception.

Along with "I spy" games play "I listen."

Internal imagery needs to be developed rather than an overload of sensory stimulation.

One of the simplest ways to do this is to introduce them to the spirit world through angels because this introduction to the spiritual realm through angels allows them to 'see' the physical body as the embodiment of the soul.

Use an egg as an example.

Tell your child that the most important part of us is inside the body just like the egg.

One day the shell will be left behind on this earth and the soul will live in a beautiful place as an Angel.

Open their mind to angels as this is the essence to imagination and morphs into the process of learning how to listen, later, this will enable them to understand the subtleties of life.

Allow young children to 'wish upon an angel" because these wishes become very meaningful when children are taught how to reflect on them, which leads to an expansion of the mind.

I have heard of three-year old children wishing that more 'flowers would grow and that the ants wouldn't get drowned by the rain.' And a slightly older child wished that all the children in the world could read because she had just started reading herself.

And because children look to us as their role models our speaking and listening should contain truth and sincerity.

This will occur naturally for us when we use the energy from within through the practice of meditation. This is when, what we perceive from our senses become spiritually motivated.

When we learn to spiritually listen every aspect of our life will improve, every situation will be accessible, and every experience will be manageable due to this internal wisdom.

Many of us have experienced the highs and lows of bringing up teenagers.

Our highs have been measured as successes while our lows have been fought with great pain and frustration and measured as failures.

All the results stem from our ability to listen.

When we 'tune-in' to our teenagers we are rewarded with the high experiences while the lows occur when communication breaks down which creates a huge void between us and them.

This happens because no one is spiritually listening.

The longer this situation is left the worse it becomes.

The listening becomes harder because it usually involves three people— both parents and the teenager.

The ideal situation is when all three persons practise meditation and use this quiet time to reflect on what each one has said.

Unfortunately, in most cases, this does not happen. But even one person intuitively listening will make a huge difference towards bringing peace and harmony into everyone's life. Spiritually listening to a troubled teenager is like looking into a mirror—just as the least change is reflected in the mirror, from a frown to the flicker of an eyelid, so too will a parent with spiritual listening observe their teenager. The energy from within will draw their attention to even the slightest change that is happening within them and then through divine guidance they will respond to their deeper needs in a more loving and nurturing manner without causing any embarrassment or resentment, or injury, to their teenager's self-esteem.

This inner wisdom will not only tell parents what their teenagers like or dislike but also why they like or dislike certain things. So often I have heard parents say,

"I had no idea that my teenager was going through such a difficult time."

Spiritual listening will create a deep empathy within parents for their teenagers instead of feelings of anger and hopelessness. A guru once told me that teenagers get knots in their hearts. This causes them to act so insensitive and selfish at times.

Parents can undo the knots by bringing out their compassionate nature, which has usually slipped so far back they have lost all sight of it.

Caring for a new pet or for a young child or an older person can bring this part of their nature back into view with positive results.

Sometimes listening to a story of struggle and hardship can stir up feelings of compassion, like this true story of Vo Thi Thang.

Some thirty years ago, while the war was on in Vietnam, Vo Thi Thang was accused of political activities. This happened regardless of whether it was the truth or not and she was sentenced to three years jail. She was sent to the island of Con Son to a prison that was notorious for its brutality where she was tortured, interrogated, and held for twelve months in a concrete tiger cage. It was topped with bars through which guards threw lime and dirty water on the prisoners and tormented them with loud noises. This last torture was aimed at preventing them from going within and finding some sort of peace and strength.

When their whole world was a nightmare even the simple need for silence was denied to them.

In an interview to journalists she said, "There were five or six women prisoners in one cell in shackles. We were never allowed out for exercise, and we had only two meals a day either plain boiled rice with salt, or rice with dried squid. They would force water into our mouth and then give us electric shocks. They would also drive nails into our fingernails and hang us upside down."

Today Vo Thi an attractive, articulate woman says, "They were difficult times, but we don't look back. We have a good life now and we look to the future."

When your teenager hears a story like this gratitude for their own good life might stir in their hearts and make them more appreciative of their parents and family around them.

Even just a flash of a thought or a momentary feeling of compassion will create a positive reaction in their mind, and this will enable them to visualize the suffering of another as opposed to themselves. It is often hard to assess how a teenager is really feeling because their moods fluctuate so rapidly.

I say to parents to promise them the world to get them meditating because the world will be their oyster if they learn to open their mind through meditation.

This will also bring their bodies back into balance-physically, emotionally, and spiritually.

Keep the meditation simple and do not allow your teenagers to experiment with any psychic activities. No Ouija boards or channelling or even trance like meditation.

I am always astounded when teenagers tell me that they have joined their parents in activities of this kind. Leave this for people who understand these transcendental practices, because these can have a physiological reaction on the body that will manifest itself through unnatural disturbances of the mind. Your only concern is with quiet and peaceful meditation that will bring peace into a troubled teenager's mind.

Jesus told his followers, "Listen—I am standing and knocking at your door. If you hear my voice, and open the door, I will come in."

Jesus was telling his audience to listen to their inner voice, and to open the door to their heart chakra so that they could experience all the goodness around them.

Just meditating on an enlightened soul's image can undo the 'knots' from your teenager's heart.

At some stage during every teenager's life, they feel explicitly drawn to some image, which could become their idol. Often it is someone in the entertainment or sporting arena, and it can become so strong, it causes them to obsessively focus a great deal of their thoughts and actions on to this image.

Provided their idol has positive characteristics this teenage experience can be a boon to them both mentally and spiritually.

How the image manages to do this magical feat without the individual coming to know what is happening to them no one can explain in explicit terms. However, these idols can cause a transformation in the teenager's psyche so they must be steered away from idols that display characteristics of depravity.

A Hindu guru told me this true story of imagery or idol-worship and its power over the mind.

Hundreds of years ago, in a far-away northern kingdom of India, there lived a young prince who had only one wish in life and that was to be a great archer. From a young age he had played constantly with his bow and arrow. Now in young adulthood the desire to excel at this skill became more dominant.

The king, wishing to please his son and heir advertised for the leading master of archery to tutor his son, regardless of cost.

Soon after, much to the prince's delight, a master archer arrived at the palace to teach the prince all he could ever want to know about archery.

The lessons began with the master soon discovering that he had an excellent student to teach, because the prince had a natural talent for archery.

One day, as the great master was setting up the targets for his royal student's lesson, a young, rather scruffy looking peasant approached him in the fields.

After humbly offering him respectful greetings he said,

"Great master, I too am an ardent lover of archery, with your kind permission would I be permitted to watch and listen whilst you teach the prince so that I too might learn some of your outstanding skills."

The master was shocked at what he perceived was sheer arrogance on the part of the peasant. How dare he even think of being in the same class as someone of princely birth!

It was unthinkable let alone permissible, so he sent the young man on his way after giving him a stern reprimand.

But this rebuke did not deter the young man in any way. He went back to his village and thought, "If I cannot go to the master then he can come to me." So, he made a clay image, that was a close replica of the archery master and placed it on a high stone where he decided to practise his archery.

With his home-made equipment he practised diligently.

In his mind the image really did become his teacher. He felt as if the image conveyed a message of praise when he performed well while messages of 'perfect your aim,' and 'steady your gaze,' came at times when his performance was not up to scratch.

Meanwhile the prince reached that level of perfection where he could, on occasions, outshine his master.

The King was so pleased with the results he ordered an Archery Contest with large sums of gold being offered to the contestants who won.

People came from all over the land to take part in the competition.

Many more came just to witness this great sporting event.

Amongst the contestants was the young peasant lad. He looked rather handsome in his borrowed clothes, and he carried a fine bow that had been made by a very skilled artisan bowyer.

The young man had befriended the bowyer who gave him newly made bows to test their flexibility and strength before he sold them to his rich clientele.

Now the young man now had one of the finest bows in his possession.

The competition finally narrowed itself down to just two contestants—the prince and the peasant. And even though the prince shot his arrows with great accuracy and speed, it was the peasant who won the tournament.

The archery master was amazed, and impressed, by the great skill of this young archer and asked him from whom had he learned such outstanding archery. Proudly the young man replied,

"From you master, because daily did your image guide me in my practice."

What the conscious mind had been denied the super conscious mind supplied.

Lead your teenager to the belief that their soul is part of the Divine soul, which is goodness personified. This is what every teenager's soul is evolving towards and it is our duty as parents to lead them towards that goal.

Try to create awareness in your teenager about their spirituality through visualizing billions upon billions of stars, crossing and re-crossing each other at countless points, filling space at every spot from end to end with their soul part of this cosmic universe, and part of the amazing ingenuity of the divine creator.

Let them understand that just as the sunshine is not the sun yet it is essentially part of it, in the same way we are part of the Divine energy.

Teenagers need to see their connection to everything in the spiritual realm.

They need to know that they are part of the marvellous super intelligent phenomena of the Universe, and that their energy is part of the cosmic vital energy on the terrestrial globe.

This information will especially appeal to the scientifically orientated teenager.

Let them see their life as a journey for the evolution of their soul just as their body, their intellect, their emotions, and their sexuality change and develop as they get older and enter adulthood, so too does their soul develop.

Encourage them to be open and honest about themselves and others and to accept all people as spiritually related, and, as such, equals on this earth planet.

Discuss acts of injustice, immorality, aggression, and hatred as unacceptable and harmful for the development of the body, mind, and soul.

If possible, get your teenagers involved in one humanitarian project. This will involve the commitment of parents too, but the benefits in the end far outweigh the cost.

Charitable programs like Freedom from Hunger, World Vision, Save the Whales or even working as a volunteer at an animal shelter are good projects to assist your teenager's spiritual growth.

Throughout this challenging time, never relinquish your role as leader even though your teenager will try every trick in the book to get you to follow them.

That remains your role because it gives them the support and strength they need during this fragile time.

Assert your leadership role lovingly and let them follow.

Through meditation and contemplation, you will be given the strength to let go when you know that they can stand up for themselves and can be held accountable for their own behaviour.

Always bear in mind through these trying years that even though talking through issues is important; speech is merely silver whilst silence is golden.

It is through silence that we get spiritual wisdom and peace of mind.

When we respect silence so too will our children.

Very often young mothers will insist upon having a lot of noise around their new baby so that the child grows up with noise and learns to live with it.

Then when they grow up parents cannot tolerate their loudness, especially their music.

When we learn to contemplate in silence, we automatically teach our children to do likewise.

Years ago, there was a beautiful song sung by Simon and Garfunkel called

'The Sound of Silence', with some of the words being:

And the vision - that was planted in my brain,

still remains, within the sound of silence.

Tell me more.

Explain the – sound of silence.

Jesus told his disciples "In the stillness of my voice I will come to thee."

Jesus is stating here that during our quiet moment, peace and tranquillity will come to us.

This is what we crave most in our lives when trauma and chaos strike.

Living with teenagers is a challenge, accept the challenge and believe, within yourself, that at the end of this journey you will become a better person, with a well-balanced offspring.

Every challenge that we accept and fulfil successfully leaves us better equipped to face future challenges in our life.

All of life is a challenge, if it were not so we would lose interest and perhaps not want to live anymore. It is the stimulation and the motivation to succeed in life that keeps most of us going, and we can only access this heightened level of enthusiasm when we use the energy from within.

The archer's energy is temporarily stored in the bow limbs and is then converted into the energy of flight through his arrow.

So too does our energy, enhanced by the Divine energy, give us strength to go forward onto our next challenge, which could very well be, for example, mid-life crisis.

For most people, the physical changes that occur in the body during the mid-life crisis can be extremely difficult to cope with. However, through meditation you can learn to listen to the rhythm of your body and be guided to seek proper help and advice. This will enable you to feel well again.

Knowledge is a wonderful asset because it gives us a better understanding of our situation, and this can change an impossible situation into a manageable one.

A hobby or an interest like yoga, to keep the body flexible, creates a diversion for the mind.

It takes our thoughts away from our physical ailments, and the enthusiasm generated for a new interest will revitalize the mind and energize the body by building healthier body cells.

The great artist Claude Monet painted some of his masterpieces after the age of 70.

It was during this time that he developed a special relationship with nature.

He found that by immersing himself into the natural environment he was able to think himself into nature more profoundly and this inspired him to paint some of his most magnificent paintings which, just to look at, cause an uplifting of the soul.

If you are not artistically inclined, try gardening because it is a real soul booster and health restorer.

Getting involved with animals can be very satisfying and therapeutic too.

Regardless of the hobby that one chooses, the key to coping and improving one's health is through meditation and the unblocking of the chakras.

This will bring peacefulness to the mind during this crucial time because the conscious mind becomes chaotic due to all the physical changes that are occurring within the body.

Often someone will approach me and say they meditate but nothing happens. They have not felt any transformation; physically, mentally, emotionally, or spiritually, and my advice is always the same—if the chakras are blocked, they will experience nothing, because regeneration of the body and mind cannot happen without the vital power of the internal energy.

Most times the blockages are caused by painful baggage people are carrying in their conscious mind.

A woman approaching her sixtieth birthday was still struggling with her painful memories of her life in an orphanage; into which she had been placed before her third birthday.

This is far too long a time for anyone to be carrying hurt and resentment.

This kind of unnecessary baggage destroys the body and mind.

She told me she talked about it often, but it still had not gone away.

Talk is no good without action and action is no good without listening.

Talk about the painful experience and then listen to what someone else has to say, or listen to yourself when you ask, "Why is this still hurting me?"

Then take the necessary action to resolve it.

This woman's husband suggested they visit the orphanage perhaps it would not look so huge any more or so dark.

Perhaps the people staying there now would appear more normal and friendly and then the new image of the orphanage could replace the old.

But the woman felt she could never return to that building so she retained the old frightening image.

The mind did not want to change the old for the new and let go of its past fear.

Changing one's patterns or beliefs is a hard to do.

Some people will hang onto the most awful things because to let it go requires change.

The energy from the Chakras cleanses everything. It is like an internal body wash.

It washes out everything that is polluted, decomposed and foul.

Sometimes there can be physical symptoms of this occurring with some people experiencing frequent bowel movements when these chakras begin to unblock during deep meditation and contemplation. Do not be alarmed by this because the body will naturally resume its normal pattern once the inner debris is expelled.

This book is primarily about unblocking the chakras for successful meditation to take place.

The practice of yoga will also increase the energy flow and thereby revitalize the body.

Life is not about suffering it is about facing up to our challenges and overcoming them successfully.

This is our journey through life, and it is our choice how we live it. We need to make the change that we want to see in our lives, which then allows us to move forward.

Some people fear they are not in control in certain situations, but we are always in control just the situation has changed, and we are presented with a different challenge.

When my son was born six weeks early, I felt out of control and it was as if my body and my baby were saying, "I'm coming, ready or not."

Then I realized I was still in control and that only the situation had changed.

So, I had to focus my mind onto my new role as a mother and allow things to fall into place naturally without allowing panic or worry to clog my mind.

Worry is an affliction of the mind. When Jack Lockett, an Australian, celebrated his one hundred and eleventh birthday, he said, "My secret to long life is not to worry."

His disposition towards life was simply amazing because he said he felt truly blessed.

When we worry about a person or a situation, we transmit negative thoughts towards that person or situation. Therefore, the possibility of a negative happening is increased.

On the other hand, when we transmit thoughts of blessings, the opposite will occur.

How many times have we heard chronic worriers say, "I was afraid that was going to happen," when something awful takes place?

Their negative thoughts created that to happen and so now the worrier has more to worry about. People who say, I prayed for that to happen, are referring to a happier and more positive outcome which ultimately gives them peace of mind.

Remember our thoughts travel through time and space and this has been proven time and again by people who say that very often they have thoughts about a particular person only to hear from that person soon after.

Lloyd John Ogilvie a professor in psychology says, "So long as we receive and therefore think thoughts of beauty, hope, cheer and courage; so long will we stay young."

John Harvey, a practitioner in mental health issues and the author of many articles of stress management had a patient come to him very worried about dying at a young age from a heart attack.

In fact, he had even convinced himself that his death would occur at the age of 48 years because, he said, "My grandfather died at 68 years and my father died at 58 years."

Harvey said "Why do you indulge in such negative thinking?

Adopt a positive attitude and a healthy lifestyle and you will live beyond even your great-grandfather."

To the best of John Harvey's knowledge, the man was alive and healthy after his 70th birthday.

The side effects from worry are too numerous to mention, but one of the worst is that parents transfer their worries onto their children, which then results in unhappy, worried children.

The worries of the parents then have a negative influence on the children.

A Hindu Sadhu once told me that there was no rebellion in children that they were only groping in the dark and that it was this darkness of their mind that caused some of them to extinguish any light or hope that came into their lives.

A young man with a drug problem, while on holiday in Bali, took a large quantity of drugs, and then in his drug-induced psychotic state jumped twice from a third-floor balcony hitting his head each time on the stone pavement below.

He then begged people to kill him.

His strength was so great no one could hold onto him.

Eventually he smashed a coke bottle and stabbed himself in the chest and died.

Some mystics believe that it is better for the embodied soul to depart to the spiritual realm before it regresses any further. Otherwise, the soul will require many more lifetimes to reach purity and oneness with the Divine.

Imagine the body, mind, and soul as a golden triangle.

When the mind is full of positive thoughts the energy from the soul becomes positively charged so it runs strongly through the triangle lighting it up with a brilliant radiance.

This visualization is the closest we can get to understanding, what occurs within our bodies.

When positive energy is generated within us people who can see auras can see this light radiating outside a person's body.

On the other hand, negative thoughts create negative energy, so the flow becomes very sluggish.

Worry weighs heavily on the mind thus little, or no light is generated.

The triangle becomes dull and cold especially after a period of despair and it is only through meditation and the unblocking of the Chakras that this energy can be activated to flow through the triangle again, to restore it to its natural brilliance.

This positive energy will then permeate the whole person to create a being of light, because, according to science, pure energy is light and heat.

This pure energy is the illumination or enlightenment of the soul.

If this vital energy is the be all and end all of everything, and if meditation is the key to unlocking this golden gate, why isn't its practice more widespread?

Why doesn't every single person on the planet participate in it?

Why has it been hidden away like some dark secret?

So, what is meditation?

Meditation is the calming down of the body and mind, into a state of utter peacefulness, unlike sleep, which is the relaxation of muscles, a decreased consciousness of the sensory organs, and a change in the pattern of the electrical activity in the brain waves, from Beta to Alpha.

Sleeping allows the body to conserve energy for later use.

The sleeper can be aroused or will wake-up after a specific duration of time.

Meditation is total relaxation of all the body parts and the brain waves go beyond Alpha to Delta, where the mind is no longer dashing about from one idea to the next.

This is different to rapid eye movement—REM, in sleep.

In meditation the control centres in the brain slow right down and switch to automatic pilot and the sensory nerves relax to such an extent they become super sensitive.

A sound will be felt as a shock when the sound vibrates on the super sensitive nerves, but it will be experienced as an internal reaction.

There will be no reaction in the brain because all the control centres will be on hold while the mind stays in this meditative state of nothingness.

Softly spoken words can bring one out of meditation or the time length planned before the meditation began will enable the person to resume normal consciousness after that specific time. During meditation, the body generates a large amount of energy unlike sleep when the energy is simply conserved.

Think of it like a cell phone when it is turned off (sleep) the energy in the battery is being conserved for later use but when it is plugged into a power point (meditation) it is creating more energy.

In very deep trance-like meditation or hibernation in sleep, the energy within the body is activated to such an extent it can create healing of tissue and body cells.

The difference between sleep and meditation can be seen as the sleep patterns of the Tree Frog and the Bull Frog, as the first is known to have a very deep sleep whilst the latter has a more alert watchful sleep.

Because opinions are divided on theories of the phenomena of sleep in this day of modern technology one can therefore understand the confusion and ignorance that abounds the subject of meditation and the state of super consciousness.

While we wait for the medical profession and scientists to conduct research into them, we will have to use the positive results from our own experiences to promote it as an essential life tool.

We cannot expect it to be promoted by the entrepreneurs of the business world, because it is not commercially viable.

One can meditate without the candles, relaxation music tapes, incense sticks, crystal balls, perfumed oils, or the purple robe because even though they assist in meditating they are not essential.

Meditation can be totally cost free and with regular concentrated practice we can release the vital life-force energy from within which is the dispensation of divine grace.

In other words, a gift from God, so man cannot profit from it because it is there to supply our needs not our wants.

The leaders of all the religious faiths practise meditation to activate this life force energy from within but years ago considered it too sacred for the common lay person.

Perhaps they thought that this exceptional divine favour was only for them because of the important role they played as bishops, priests, or monks.

We do know that in years past reading the Bible and other sacred texts was the privilege of only religious leaders.

Ordinary folk had to hope that what was preached to them was done in honesty and truth. However, in many instances this was not the case, which in turn led to widespread antagonistic feelings towards religious practices.

Meditative worship programs will give everyone an opportunity to reach spiritual enlightenment through loving spiritually.

I call it the W.C.S. program—it is when we wisely, care and share with our fellow humans and all other living things on this planet.

It is called intuitive compassion.

Caring and sharing without wisdom results in wasted energy and resources.

For example, there is no point in giving or/sharing your money with a person who has a drinking problem; because they will just take that money and drink it. Wisdom will show you other avenues of help that you can give them.

This is the wisdom from within, that develops in us noble character traits.

There was an advertisement for cigarettes many years ago and it referred to the pleasure of smoking as a sterling experience.

We of course know that they were being totally dishonest in that advertisement because many smokers experienced only a morbid time of pain and death from lung cancer.

But a sterling experience or having sterling qualities is the result of inner wisdom and when people vibrate with the joy of life it becomes contagious.

This is how it is when we wisely care and share.

All our life experiences end up having an element of success attached to them.

One of the saddest things in our society today is the addiction to drugs by our young people.

It radically alters once beautiful children, who lose their cognitive faculty in the search for abnormal ecstasy.

They live in a world of sorrow and pain, and the effect of the narcotics on the mind and body are devastating. Their existence revolves around feeding their drug habit, which they become so dependent upon it causes them to lose all purpose in life to the point where the consideration of others is totally lost sight of, and they reach the lowest level of utter selfishness.

I have seen parents give so much in a desperate effort to help save their children from destroying their young lives. Amongst these parents I have witnessed the highest peak of sacrifice.

It is a constant battle to try and set their child on the correct path again.

What causes these teenagers, and other young people to turn to drugs to feel fulfilled? Therapists have blamed society, family background, lack of education and the availability of drugs.

However, there is no correct answer as to why?

Yes, feelings of abandonment, low self-esteem and other emotional issues do aggravate the problem, but they are not the cause of the problem.

The answer to why teenagers take drugs is far more complex.

On my last visit to India my friend had offered temporary accommodation to a young couple from a remote village.

The young wife was heavily pregnant and on the day of my arrival she gave birth to a baby boy. The birth of a child is so uplifting that it was a lovely start to my holiday.

The young woman's mother-in-law took care of her and the new baby whom she held to her bare stomach often for three days, while the mother stayed in a meditative state on her bed and was fed a type of broth made from lentils and vegetables.

When I asked the young mother why she was not allowed to leave her bed or care for her *baby* for three days the mother-in-law promptly answered,

"She has just given birth, that puts a lot of strain on the mother physically, mentally and emotionally. Now she needs to rest and meditate, and the soul (Atman) will bring everything back into balance."

"What about feeding the baby?" I asked.

"No," said mother-in-law, "the baby is fine the mother must think only of herself for three days."

"Wouldn't the baby dehydrate, and what about the colostrum in the mother's milk? "

"That will still be there after the third day," was the mother-in-law's reply.

As for the new baby, well he had to get the rhythm of the breath right first.

The mother-in-law was adamant that the breath was everything.

The breath was life and if the body got that right, then everything else would follow suit.

She said it took twenty-four hours for the rhythm of the breath to get right and whilst that was happening the body was not to be distracted with feeding and digesting and bowel and bladder functions.

My next question was "Why three days, if the rhythm of the breath was established after the first day why the extra two days."

Her answer was, "Because that's how long it takes sometimes for the aura to be complete in a new life."

She went on to say that if their aura, was not fully formed, the child would never truly belong to earth in this life-time, their soul would always want to leave.

We do not know how long it takes for the aura to be complete after birth, but we do know that if it is prevented from maturing that person is locked into self-destructive patterns.

This could be the reason why so many of our young people find it so hard to settle down in this world,

I know, at times, we all have a yearning to be elsewhere, in another more peaceful world. However, for some people the yearning is greater than their desire to live here on earth.

Does this lead them towards the destruction of their bodies so the soul can return to its original home?

Can there be any truth or deeper wisdom in these ancient beliefs?

Perhaps our Aura consultants can shed some light in this area?

Incidentally, Grandma did give the new baby some diluted goat's milk after the first day.

Just a few drops in the mouth every few minutes no sucking or a full feed till after the third day when Mum rose from the bed full of energy! She was collecting sticks and chopping wood and looked fantastic.

When I visited four months later the baby was thriving and mum was beaming.

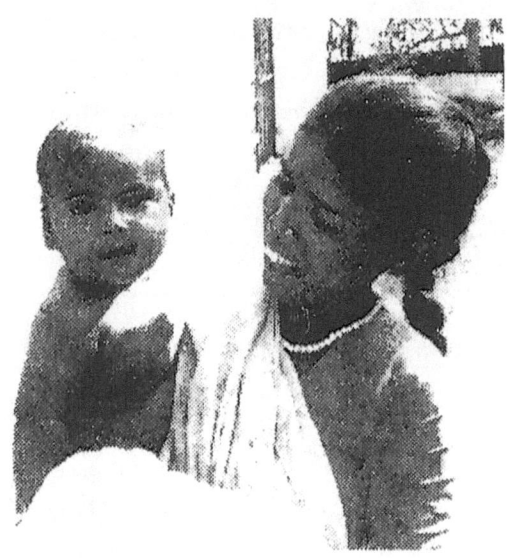

Whatever the cause for drug addiction, whether it be physical, mental or an ethereal affliction, the practice of meditation in an isolated caring environment—an ashram is good for this—has a good chance of treating the addiction successfully.

When the normal powers of the mind are unable to stop the addiction, the super conscious mind can help to eradicate the drug problem from the addict's life.

However, we know that this wrestling with the mind is no *easy* task.

The mind will keep insisting that the drug is needed and that it is vital for survival.

Intellectually, the drug user knows that this is not the case, quite the opposite in fact, but they cannot stop the addiction.

The mind is powerful, and whilst it is craving abnormal ecstasy the soul is longing for peace and calm and wellness of body. So, a power struggle takes place in the drug addicts' life between their human nature and their spiritual nature.

There are days when they truly feel they can kick the habit.

These are the times when they feel spiritually strong.

It is at these times that a drug user needs to tune-in to their super conscious mind by imagining their soul as a sterling silver sword emitting rays of light and fighting the forces of evil (drugs); in much the same way that St. George fought the dragon of wickedness.

According to English folklore, George was a courageous and honest young man, pure of heart, who saved a small English town from being destroyed by an evil dragon.

Legend has it that, one day, when the women of the hamlet went to draw water from a nearby pool a huge dragon emerged from its depths and sent them all running back to the safety of their walled town.

But the fire-breathing dragon pursued them and tried to use its powerful body to knock down the wall and the gates. It was only after the women of the hamlet had satisfied its hunger by giving it two sheep to eat did it retreat to the depths of the pool.

But the next day the dragon returned for more food—and then the next day and then the next. The people were now more concerned than ever before.

"What will happen when there are no more sheep to feed the dragon?" they asked one another.

So, they started to draw lots as to who would go as food for the dragon.

This caused immense pain and suffering in everyone's heart and left people totally devastated. Then one day the Princess' name was picked out as food for the dragon.

She was sent to the place where the dragon came daily to eat its food.

Just as she was about to be devoured by the dragon a young man named George arrived on a white horse and what he saw horrified him.

A bloodied battle ensued between George and the dragon.

One version of the story stated that he slew the dragon, whilst another said he tamed it.

This is a story of good overcoming evil.

The story was kept alive for over a thousand years, and then, one day a group of English soldiers, weary from battle, witnessed a glorious sight of George on his white horse, holding his special banner in front of him.

It was this vision that made George the patron saint of England.

And just as St. George used his sword to fight his dragon, drug addicts need to use creative visualization to consolidate this image in their mind of their sword that has no limitations in time, place, or strength to fight this evil habit.

Only use the sword to fight the drugs never another person.

Not the pushers or dealers, or the manufacturers nor the chemicals or plants used in the making of them. This fight is with the drugs, this is what is hurting the bodies and minds of people.

This is the culprit, so the sword attacks just that—the drugs, until they are totally eradicated from the mind.

In other words, it is the craving for the drugs in the minds of drug addicts that need to be destroyed.

Therefore, the answer to the world's drug problem is to find a way to stop the craving.

The source of the problem is right there, within the mind of every drug user.

How the mind got into this state is debatable.

It could be due to genetic factors, or it could be physical, mental, emotional, or spiritual abnormalities.

More research is required in all these areas before the cause can be accurately identified—then they will come to a dead-end because how does one assess spiritual abnormalities?

It is our natural tendency when trying to deal with the devastation of drugs on our fellow human beings to go out and get the drug dealer or destroy the plants that are grown to feed their habit. We demolish the factories and backyard laboratories making these drugs.

But instead, we should be using all our resources to stop the craving for the drug.

This is our immediate task.

We should begin with the first link in the chain but instead we rush off and try to control the supplier only to discover that when this avenue is located and shut down another one pops up immediately.

Like a dog chasing its tail it never quite gets it.

What we need to be fighting is the internal craving for drugs, that irrepressible desire for the drug-induced experience which leaves these poor tortured souls in an awful predicament of fear and aversion.

They are left devoid of feelings of love and compassion, and veneration for the divine and the wellness of their planet, because their focus is fixed firmly on their desire to get more drugs.

If there are glimpses of their true loving nature rising to the fore the mind will immediately destroy these thoughts and take them back to the obsessive craving for drugs.

The mind does not give them a chance to change.

We can change this addiction of the mind through meditation.

If you looked at the surface of the brain you would see a complicated mass of nerve cells that are connected by a network of nerves to all parts of the body.

This amazing network of pathways carries about three million messages between the brain and the rest of the body every second!

In this way all parts of the body and brain talk to each other.

The brain has several control centres that decode the messages and then decide what action to take. Some of the control centres work automatically, for example we do not have to think about breathing the control centre makes sure we do it, but if we want to hold our breath, we can only take control for a short time.

Meditation gives us control of the control centres in the brain, and the first centre to focus on and master is the breath.

At first, this is quite difficult to do. Why?

Because the control-centre in the brain wants to do the job automatically, you are changing the pattern.

Begin with breathing slowly and rhythmically, stay focused on just the breath. If you find your attention wandering bring it back again and again to the rhythm of the breath whenever it moves in any other direction.

Try to constantly increase the intensity of concentration.

Next try to change the rhythm of the breath. Take a very deep breath then let it out very slowly. Focus on this for a while then repeat the exercise several times.

Then change the rhythm to short sharp breaths, in and out in and out.

Now go back to your normal breathing pattern.

This will make your brain happier because you have given control back to it.

The brain is quite happy to change the rhythm of the breath when it wants to, like, when we are running it is quick. When we are frightened, we hold onto it.

But all these instructions come from the control centre, not from us consciously.

When you sit in a chair totally relaxed and you change the rhythm of the breath to very heavy breathing the control centre says,

"I'm in charge, I want the rhythm to be slow and regular," but you go ahead and change it using your power of control.

This is when you are truly in touch with your body.

At the end of the day, it is your body, and you are responsible for it.

On the facing page is a simple diagram of the control centres of the brain.

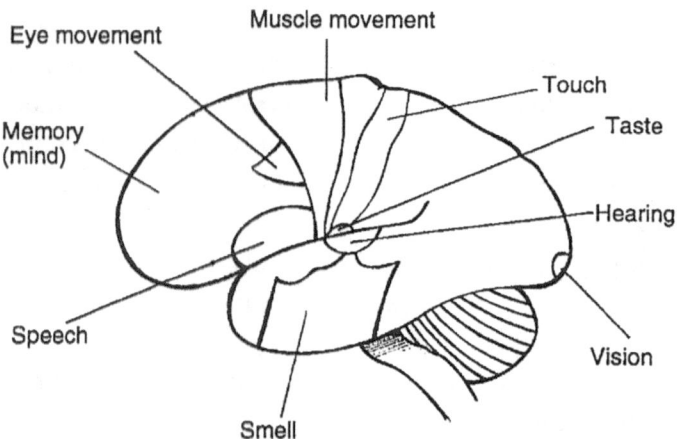

If we study it closely, we will see that the largest control centre is the mind, therefore our memories are the major control centre in the mind.

When we consciously control all these centres, from hearing to muscle-movement, we can control the mind too and, therefore, stop the addictions.

Experiment with a few more.

Take an orange, cut it in half and put your nose right up to it but do not smell it.

Keep breathing though.

This is a difficult exercise to do because you need to keep your mind concentrating on anything else other than the smell of the orange.

It will desperately want you to smell the orange, however, you say, "I am not going to smell it." Before you put the orange down be kind and have a good smell of it, if you want to, to keep the mind happy.

Listen to some music.

While it is still on shift your concentration elsewhere, consciously refuse to listen to the music. Even that split second that you did not hear the music puts you in control.

It is possible to consciously divorce your mind from your senses.

The capacity of the human brain is staggering, but you need to have some control over it.

This is the conscious control of the mind that can be achieved through focussed concentration, and when taken further will bring us a fleeting glimpse of that power-house of all knowledge, the super conscious mind.

Countless hymns have been written praising this transforming prowess within the human-body, of going from the conscious state, into the super conscious state, that can be achieved through meditation.

My greatest wish is that all parents teach their children how to meditate from an early age, and to see it introduced into places of learning.

This skill would be the most valuable thing any child could learn.

Maureen Garth, who has done a lot of research in this area, says,

"Children would benefit greatly from learning the art of meditation."

Make meditation your vocation and each time you meditate imagine, visualize, you are on vacation, and while you are on this exotic vacation feel the regenerative and transformative processes at work in your body.

After the meditation you will feel refreshed; because in meditation the mind is slowed down so complete rest occurs, and this allows our often agitated, overworked mind to become an ocean of bliss.

Some people after meditating cannot speak for a few seconds. That is because the control centre for speech is located near the mind centre and the process of radically slowing the mind down effects the next centre as well.

In the same way the eyes will also stay fixed for a few seconds after deep meditation because of its closeness to the mind centre.

The listening stays intact though because at this point it is supersensitive.

Sometimes you might notice children staring into space with no eye movement.

Some people call it daydreaming, but they are meditating.

Whilst in this meditative state they should never be suddenly startled or spoken to loudly, because the electrical signals which pass from one nerve cell to another is very acute, and it can make them physically jump, just as if they have had an electric shock.

With someone who is addicted to drugs or medication, the memory control centre registers pain or a craving for the drug and remembers the release of that craving or pain when the drug is taken, so the person feels totally compelled to obey the will of the mind.

Everything in the body focuses on getting that drug and as soon as it is given to the body the mind registers, "No more pain, this is good, I feel release."

This is the message the brain sends to the rest of the body, and they travel along nerves at an incredible speed.

The message from a kiss travel at an amazing 225 kmph.

Therefore, the message 'this is good' after a drug has been taken, from the mind to the brain is instant.

We know the message 'this is good' is untrue because the drug is not good for the body, so the conscious mind is lying.

The brain, through our senses, often confuses us.

Look at this object, how many prongs does it have?

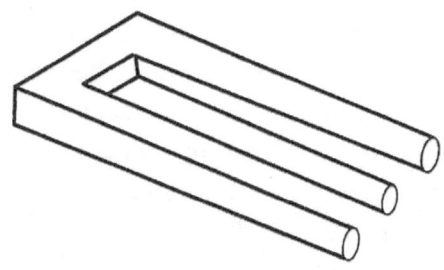

This is an optical illusion.

In the same way a lot of messages that travel to the mind in the brain are illusions.

This real-life experience will authenticate this last statement.

On a farm in Mackay, Queensland, Australia, a young farmer's wife had her right arm severed, from the shoulder, when it got caught in a post hole digging machine in a freak accident.

Even though she has made a remarkable recovery, Gayle still has days when the pain is overwhelming.

One of the biggest burdens is the so-called, phantom pain.

The orthopaedic specialists say the way the accident happened affects the pain you get.

She said "I'm getting pain which feels like my fingers are bending back really hard.

They say that might have been my last memories of the pain."

Here we have a disabled woman minus a right arm getting severe pain from fingers she no longer has!

Even though this woman's pain is from a different source to that of the drug addicts' pain, it is nonetheless a deceptive pain that is registering in the conscious mind.

Whom do we trust: our mind, or our inner voice?

Meditation gives us clarity to see the true picture. We understand what is real and what is not which at times causes an inexplicable alteration to the very depths of our personality.

How often have we heard someone say, "I can't believe the change in that person?"

This is especially true of former drug addicts who from the lowest state of selfishness have changed and become the pillars of society.

Through meditation we can change any deep-rooted disturbances of the mind.

Whatever the unhealthy and harmful craving might be, whether it be for drugs, alcohol, cigarettes or gambling, meditation can change the thoughts of the mind from please, give me that drug, to, I do not need them anymore.

It is as simple as that.

But it is a slow process because to alter the mind requires strength and determination.

When we choose what thoughts we put into our mind, and what actions we make, we have mastery over the mind.

Buddha said, "Right thoughts lead to right action."

When we begin to think positively, we will get an enlarged picture of the world.

Not enlarged in the sense of magnification by a microscope, but by a wider perception of our environment, and then the knowing of our self will acquire extended proportions.

The emphasis will shift from, what can I do to get what I want? To, what can I do to make this world a better place for everyone?

When we Care and Share wisely, we will be carrying our mind upwards, towards a higher consciousness.

Our intuitive listening guides us to use our time and energy on tasks that, apart from helping others, will be beneficial to our own spiritual welfare.

Giving a helping hand that leaves us feeling frustrated and used, due to the hang-ups we carry in our unconscious mind by the dominance of others, usually parents, will not occur, because we will feel no pressure or obligation to help in those situations.

The wisdom from the super conscious mind will show us how to overcome feelings of being coerced into doing things we do not need to do and lead us to do jobs that are helpful and fulfilling. So, when someone says, "Thank you for your help", we will honestly be able to say, "It's been a pleasure."

This is one of the greatest benefits of inner listening - we never fall into the category of being used, which ultimately leads to a feeling of resentment.

It does not matter how onerous a task is because it is worth every ounce of the effort when it brings an expansion of our consciousness.

Hindu gurus say this is the merging of the little Self, our conscious and unconscious mind, with the Supreme Self, the super conscious mind.

OUR INTERNAL ENERGY ENERGISED, THE CHAKRAS UNFOLDED

Most people's journey through life is one of suffering and joy. Our aim is to decrease the suffering and increase the joyfulness, and this can only be achieved through the rising of the ambrosial current within us.

This is sometimes called the divine source or universal energy, or power of the Holy Spirit (Christianity) or Kundalini (Hinduism) or Secret energy of the Golden Flower (Taoist) or thousand petals Lotus (Buddhism).

It has been given many names, but the gift and the experience are the same, irrespective of what religious leaders preach, or what scientists teach.

Science has come a long way we now know that our Sun is one of billions of stars in the galaxy and that it converts six hundred million tons of hydrogen into helium every second and has been doing so for more than four billion years.

Scientists now tell us that every atom in our bodies, the heavier ones being in our bones, was present in stars billions of years ago!

We know that everything on earth is made up of millions upon millions of atoms. Energy is released when atoms split or undergo fission. When it splits into two it releases energy as light, heat, and radiation.

It also produces neutrons, tiny particles of the split atom, which causes fission in other atoms, to cause a chain reaction. The energy released when a chain reaction occurs is enormous.

In the same way when these chakras are energized, they produce their own electromagnetic field of light like a laser beam. Science has already shown us that a laser beam is a beam of very pure light which is so powerful it can drill a tiny hole in a diamond, slice through steel plates, and help in delicate surgical operations.

This pure light of divine energy gives us the energy and vitality to heal our bodies and enables us to cope well in traumatic situations. In other words, it makes us more powerful; but to activate this energy, it is essential to keep these chakras open to receiving and expressing this life-force vital energy. We have the choice to use it or lose it.

It is like controlling the brain centres, but unlike the brain they are not yet visible to the intellectual mind. However, as scientific research reveals more and more of the workings of the human brain perhaps, in the, not too distant future, these energy centres too will be revealed to the intellectual mind.

For the moment though we will have to content ourselves with personal experiences and the mystical beliefs of the ancient sacred texts.

We do know that some fish, sharks for example, can detect the inner energy of other fish.

This energy that fish can see in other fish must be like our own chakra energy, even though humans cannot see this energy in each other.

According to ancient Hindu belief the energy centres connected to our body are called Chakras.

There are seven major chakras, depicted as seven wheels, each one a different colour, like those of the rainbow. They rotate to create light and release life-force energy into the body via the spinal cord.

Brahmin sadhus, holy men, whilst in deep trance-like meditation witnessed through their inner-vision seven circular pools of moving energy as part of their body.

Each chakra was emitting rays of coloured light identical to those of the rainbow.

They saw it in the same way that some people see auras—rays of coloured light extending externally from the body, sometimes in the form of a halo.

Sadhus witnessed these vortexes of energy and light spiralling into the body, with its circular motion taking on the appearance of a wheel, like a luminous revolving disc, where thick clusters of nerves were situated.

We know that the colours of a rainbow are formed when rays of light bend at different angles within raindrops. In the same way the chakra colours are formed by the radiating currents of light and energy like those of the light spectrum, from red to violet.

When we control these energy centres, this control being in the form of keeping these chakra centres open to the divine energy, we will receive internal purification.

This converted pure energy will bring our body, mind, and soul into balance with everything that is within us, and around us.

When we consciously make the effort to keep our thoughts and actions pure, the Divine energy will replenish and revitalize these energy centres, and life here on earth will not be a burden.

Let us visualize this Divine energy as a huge and almighty river, unimaginable in its size and volume, with its source way up in the crystal-clear heavens, and with each one of us being blessed with seven tributaries leading from this source of infinitely pure iridescent clear water. This is the water of life that cleanses us and refreshes our souls. But what would happen if our tributaries got blocked due to pollution, unclean thoughts, and actions; debris, burdens as heavy as logs and rocks; or erosion, when materialism erodes our true values?

The flow of water from the almighty river will cease, and our tributaries, our streams of living water, would dry up.

They would become lifeless because without the supply from the main source there will be nothing left to flow on.

So too it is within us – if these Chakras, wheels of light, are blocked the divine cosmic energy, water, cannot flow into us – we have chosen to shut it off or have done nothing to keep the flow open.

It is either a case of reject or neglect. Either way we are to blame.

The good news is that this situation is reversible.

The main source, that almighty river, is still there waiting for us to clear the blockages so it can flow through us freely again.

And sometimes the flow is even stronger the second time around with the streams of spiritual water, energy, overflowing into every aspect of our lives so we can experience true peace and happiness. This is the transformation of psycho-physical energy into spiritual energy.

This next chapter is an attempt to bring to your conscious mind an understanding and awareness of our chakra energy system and our connection to the brilliant, illuminating universal energy of the Divine.

According to ancient Sanskrit texts, the chakras are wheels of light that narrow as they spiral into our body in front of and along the spinal column and belong to our central nervous system.

Over the years they have been interpreted and explained by many Hindu gurus including Swami Vivekananda, who was referred to as a genius.

Once, before giving a lecture at Harvard University, Professor Wright introduced him as, "a person more learned than all our learned men put together."

This diagram will help you to visualize where these energy centres are.

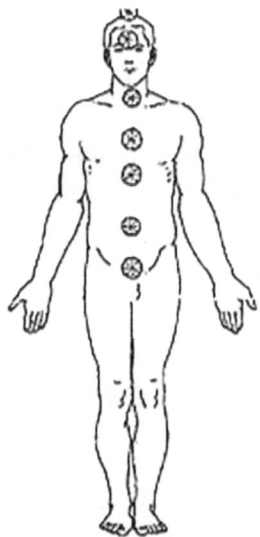

The lowest energy centre Muladhara, is represented by the colour Red and is located at the base of the spine.

To keep this energy centre unblocked we need to reconnect with the Earth.

We need to fit into our environment instead of trying to change the environment to suit our unrealistic wants. When we care for our environment the benefits to us are immeasurable.

In the movie, *The Blue Planet,* we can see the devastation humankind has done to our planet. Mountains, forests, lakes, and rivers have been totally eradicated in some places.

When we reflect on how humans have changed our planet, we feel a sense of hurt and sadness. Why? Because our energy is part of the Earth's magnetic energy. The depletion of the Earth's energy is ultimately a loss of our own energy. That is why we feel sadness when this energy is drawn from us.

The energy from the Muladhara chakra allows us to see all of nature as our friend; we see it as part of us and in us. We realize that when we harm nature, we are really harming ourselves that the fragility of the land is our own frailness, and the insecurities of our wildlife are our own insecurities.

The land gives us our strength, not just physically in the form of food, but spiritually too through this chakra. That is why working with nature is so uplifting. When we walk barefoot or touch the dirt with our hands, we physically connect to an external part of ourselves. Keep this chakra open by creating your own garden, or work as a volunteer in a public park or garden.

Projects like, Save the Rain forests, Stop Oil Pollution in our Oceans and No more Uranium Mines, are excellent to become involved with. These projects protect our planet and everyone who takes an active part in promoting this awareness is blessed because the vibrant thankful energy from the earth flows abundantly through their Muladhara Chakra.

This keeps them grounded to earth, so they can stand strong through all of life's experiences. When we work together to preserve our natural heritage, we are preserving all life on our planet. The earth's survival is in our hands not in anyone else's, not in its Creator. It is our responsibility to ensure its survival. The assumption, so long as it is here while I am still alive is an illusion. Reincarnation states that we will all need this earth again and again for our earthly existences. Besides, we need to unselfishly consider our children and our grandchildren and our great grandchildren's future home. So, we need to protect it for eternity.

There is a connection between the Muladhara chakra and the colour red in the Australian Aboriginal flag which represents the Earth. From the Earth the Aborigines used a red powder called ochre to paint on bark and rocks, this action was to create a positive reaction to the energy of this chakra. Sometimes this ochre was mixed with water to represent blood in symbolic rites. In Christianity red wine is symbolically used in the sacred ritual of the Mass because it was drunk by Jesus and his followers just before his crucifixion. It is seen as the blood of Christ to purify the energy within through the Divine's love and mercy. Because this chakra represents nature the planting and cultivation of the vines and the process of making wine involving interaction of people with the earth further enhances the energy of the Muladhara chakra. In this way the drinking of red wine in moderation can be beneficial to the body because of the nutrients in the wine. For the mind, it releases tension and for the soul it unblocks the flow of energy from this chakra.

This Muladhara Chakra is also connected to the survival of our species and to that of all animal species on earth. To hinder this natural cycle of life in any way blocks this chakra. The sexual act is considered a sacred act because it signifies the two life forces of male and female coming together from a need to create life; as it is seen in all of nature as the seed, semen, being planted in the Earth, womb, to grow. This union of male and female is also seen as the cosmic energy of Yin and Yang in Chinese principles. To further emphasize this miracle in the womb Hindu's build shrines near their temples called the Garbhagriha, womb-house. In these dark round rooms new mothers offer thanks to the God of nature for their birth-giving, natural, experience. Many years ago, new Christian mothers had to go to church to be cleansed after giving birth. An aunt of mine recalled how she had to wait outside the church covered in a long veil while the priest said the 23rd Psalm. Her only response was "Deliver us from evil" then only was she allowed to lift the veil and enter the church and participate in the worship program. She believed that covering her face with the veil was to cover the shame of the sexual act that created her baby.

Once she was cleansed and forgiven for that 'shameful' act, she was welcomed back into the church. In Hinduism, the sexual act is seen as a sacred act because it promises the continuity of human beings as God's creation and humankind's fulfilment of that promise. It is common to see images carved from hard stone of the yoni-lingam, female, and male genitals, in Hindu temples. The Yoni signifies the life-force of fertility which is the birth-giving nature of the female, while the Lingam symbolizes a manifestation on the earthly planet of the male cosmic energy being released, from his ego capsule, to experience that state of being, which links him with the- all. In relation to this chakra, the sexual act for the male is one of humbleness; as he releases his ego, he seeks to restore unity of beings, as opposed to fragmentation of the species. For the female it is more than the purpose of reproduction, it must be an act to strengthen the emotional attachment between human beings; it is seen as a nurturing of our species to a higher level of consciousness

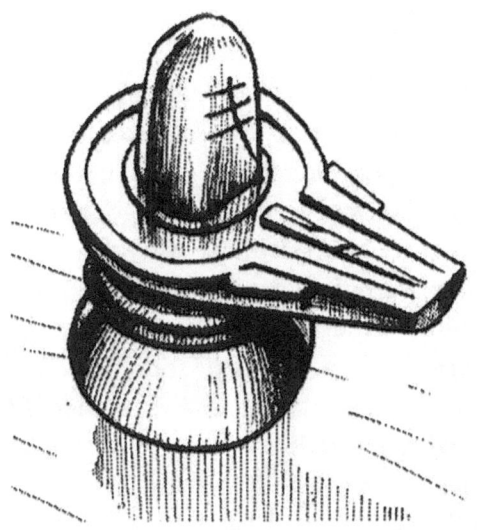

A friend of mine in India was given this stone image as a wedding present. According to her belief it represented her fertility, which was a gift from Brahman that brought about a state of oneness in her family and home. Another friend of mine, a Catholic, received a crystal statue of the Virgin Mary holding the Christ child as a wedding present. It reminded her of God's love in her family and home. Each image was important to the persons concerned because it reflected how they visualized their belief in the family unit. Both are seen as sacred, because they represent two different cultural views of the blessing of fertility.

This Chakra is enhanced during the sexual act not just for the purpose of conception, but also for construction because it helps to build a complete personality. This happens when it is participated in with the mutual consent, respect, and love, of the persons concerned. There is no distinction made between heterosexual couples or homosexual couples because it is viewed as an act to attain self-realization, which brings unity and stability to the conscious mind.

In Western culture people use red images and objects to represent love and sexuality, there are- red love hearts red roses and red clothing.

The Kama Sutra, Hindu book, is very explicit in explaining how to keep this chakra activated. Here it states that the more satisfaction given during the sexual act, the greater the benefits for the giver, unlike the Christian faith which saw it mainly as an act to conceive children.

Tantra Yoga involves yoga exercises to tone up the body to enhance muscular suppleness and to improve breathing and the sense of rhythm so that during sexual intercourse all tension and stress can be released. The sexual act then brings a state of bliss to the body, mind, and soul. It is called Chakra puja, puja meaning sacred ritual, when it is inspired by the powerful emotions of karma, which means a good action, pure sex, results in a better rebirth. It seems appropriate to add here—'As you sow, so shall you reap', because on the opposite scale of positive, healthy sexual intimacy, there is the unhealthy, impure physical act of sexual activity, that which is harmful to oneself and others. When the sexual act causes one to feel angry or hurt or ashamed it means that instead of this act of unity opening this Mulaldhara chakra it shuts it down.

Instead of a feeling of spiritual and physical growth there is a feeling of decay and death because the Inner-Self dies with the hurt and shame, whether consciously or unconsciously. That is why people who have been sexually abused and the abusers find it almost impossible to unblock this chakra. They have suicidal and unloved feelings until the energy of this chakra is flowing again. Meditation, with helpful counselling, will unblock this chakra. And with patience and forgiveness the faith in themselves and others will be restored. The energy from this chakra will then help them to forgive and move onto more fulfilling relationships.

The energy created from this chakra when conception occurs is awesome, and for some pregnant women it creates a widening of their consciousness due to the new life in their womb, hence the visible 'glow' in most pregnant women—it is the Muladhara chakra working to capacity. New father's-to-be experience the same increase of energy with more strength and vigour, and greater sensations in the reproductive organs.

Soon after birth Hindu babies are tied with the sacred thread around their bodies. It usually consists of six threads with a knot at one end. The six threads represent the first six Chakras with the knot representing the seventh chakra.

Children that are nurtured and loved begin adulthood with an unblocked Muladhara chakra, and it is easier for them to keep it this way throughout their lives. On the other hand, children who have had traumatic lives, begin adulthood with a blocked Muladhara chakra, this causes them to have a lot of relationship problems.

Some sadhus believe that a blocked Muladhara chakra causes a man to become sterile.

This chakra is the biological basis of the development and evolution of the personality. The genetic make-up of the child, that it inherits from its biological parents, along with the child's upbringing and cultural background, including their religious aspirations, exercises the greatest influence in the evolution of their soul. Whether it moves on to a higher state of consciousness or regresses depends upon the flow of energy from this first chakra because it is the key to building up a strong personality.

The first three chakras are tied to our human nature while the last three help us to reach enlightenment. The fourth chakra, in the middle of the seven major chakras, is our link between the two. Hindu Sadhus say that an unblocked Muladhara chakra will help clear any blockages from the next two chakras and that when these three lower chakras are working, they create a very successful human being.

The Sanskrit name for the second energy centre is Svadisthana, and it is located just below the navel, our first connection point to another human being through the umbilical cord.

The colour radiating from this energy vortex is predominately orange, the second colour of the rainbow.

This orange chakra is related to our interaction with humankind. To be born pre-supposes our relationships and our connection in the community. It begins with our relationships in the family, then moves on to the community, bonding us to our friends at school and at work. From here it flows onto the people of our country, and is why, many people who work or live overseas feel instinctively drawn to people from their own country. Finally, we reach out to everyone in the world because we feel connected to each other spiritually. This wider interaction brings an expansion to the mind and an evolution of the soul.

The 'orange people' from the hippy era, preached about our connection to one another.

They even wore orange clothing to emphasize this connection. Today, due to even more globalization and our vast access to modern technology we can connect with people all over the world; and with the high level of marriage break down it is quite common for children and adults to be part of a large extended family.

Good strong, relationships, increases the flow of energy from this chakra.

Sometimes, after a painful breakup from a relationship or friendship, it is difficult to feel connected to anyone else again. The hurt and the deception can be a deterrent to any future partnerships but closing ourselves off from others closes this chakra too, and then we are denying ourselves the possibility of a fulfilling relationship with someone else. After a sad break-up work extra hard with this chakra to keep the energy flowing wear orange clothes and light orange candles, invite people over, visit people, go out and socialize, because the energy from the Svadisthana chakra will restore trust back into your belief system. Then you will be able to happily move forward wisely caring and sharing with others.

The Svadisthana chakra develops trust in individuals, and it gives us the power to move away from untrustworthy people who, due to this blocked energy, have not yet discovered truth.

When I was living in Seoul, South Korea, I made a conscious effort to interact with the local people as much as possible. One Sunday, at a Christian church, I met a young Korean woman, who was interested in Australia and was eager to learn about the country, so I invited her around to my house. The next day she phoned me and thanked me for my hospitality and asked me if I would like to go shopping with her, I agreed, and we had a delightful time together because she was constantly laughing. After seeing her regularly for a couple of weeks she asked me whether she could bring her four-year-old orphan niece to my house. I immediately said, "Yes", and that I would enjoy having a little girl around to play with my two boys. The three of them played happily together even though she could not speak English and they could not speak Korean. A few days later my new Korean friend phoned and asked if I could keep the little girl for the next weekend because she had to visit a sick relative and could not take the child with her. I felt happy to help, and so the little girl was left with me on the Friday.

The weekend passed without any word from my new friend, so I thought perhaps something had held her up and she had been unable to contact me. On Monday I phoned her place but there was no answer. By Wednesday I was getting a bit concerned because I still had had no word from her. Then, that evening some policemen arrived at my house and demanded to see the child, and in extremely limited English, they told me that they were arresting me for kidnapping a Korean child and for trying to take her out of the country! They said I had to accompany them down to the Police Station immediately with the child.

I was not even allowed to make a phone call. My husband was away at the time, so I left my boys with the maid and accompanied the policemen to the station. I had been led to believe the child had no parents, but the father of the little girl was waiting there, he had reported her missing the day before and a search had been conducted to find her, which had eventually led to my house. After six hours at the police station, I discovered that this Korean woman was a wanted person on many extortion charges. She would 'borrow' a young child and then leave the child with someone she assumed would be interested in adopting an 'orphaned' Korean child. She would ask for a thousand dollars for the paper-work to be processed and while the paper-work was being processed she would request to take the child out to buy them a special gift, and, of course, she would not return with the child!

My case was a bit different from the others because I had never discussed adopting the child, neither had I given her any money. She operated in a similar way with the child's parents—she would befriend them and then offer to take care of one of the children for a few days. But this time when she did not return the child to the parents they went to the police, who immediately checked all the expatriates in the city and came to visit me.

We left Seoul soon after that 'kidnapping' incident so I never did find out whether that Korean woman was ever found and arrested. All I could do was pray for her and hope that she would leave her path of lies and deception and choose a new path of healing and honesty. Through my practice of meditation, I became more selective in choosing friends overseas and today I have some wonderful friends all over the world.

The energy from the Svadisthana chakra keeps trust flowing between people with the added blessing of discernment. It is a sad fact of life that some people cannot be trusted, but it is vital that through our example these people learn to honour trustworthiness. And we too need to constantly strive to remain honest and trustworthy in all our dealings with others. The energy from this chakra will allow us to know who is trustworthy and who needs to learn some lessons in trustworthiness.

This chakra increases our intuitiveness—to put it bluntly we get that 'gut' feeling more often.

Little children are so trusting of adults, they come into this world feeling safe with older people, so it is sad when adults abuse that trust; when children are hurt or neglected in anyway by adults, they grow up finding it hard to trust others. They are unable to use the energy from this centre due to their inability to connect with others.

Having the trust of others gives us self-respect which leads on to loving, fulfilling relationships.

The energy from the Svadisthana chakra destroys the ego that part of us that keeps us distanced from other people, because it is our ego that is constantly striving to prove that we are better than others. It hinders us from interacting with people from all walks of life. People with money like to believe that their wealth makes them superior to others, while others think they are more intellectual and so cannot connect with those who are lesser educated. Our ego even prevents us from interacting with people from other countries because it gives us an exaggerated misconception that ethnic people are inferior to us. This is especially evident amongst different religious beliefs, where each religious group strives to prove how much more infallible their faith is compared to everyone else's faith and then loving our neighbour as our self becomes entirely absent. The energy from this luminous orange chakra destroys the ego and we truly do begin to love our neighbour as our self, which unblocks this chakra.

One of the worst examples of egotism was when one nation conquered another through deception or brutal force and then, completely, destroyed their way of life. They took it upon themselves to completely change the indigenous people's way of life to comply with their 'superior' form of living—language, food, clothing, behaviour and even their beliefs were changed. This happened when the English ruled India and when the Spanish invaded Peru and when the Dutch took over Africa and is how the Chinese treat the Tibetans. Each new settler believed their way was better than the original inhabitants and this destroyed the trust between human-beings. This lack of trust all around the globe has led to the overall destruction of self-respect for the indigenous people, which collectively destroyed the divine source of love from flowing freely amongst all people.

No one could trust anyone anymore; people became egocentric, in other words they thought only of their own interests and feelings, which, when left unchecked can spread like a virus into egomania. That is when a whole country of people become obsessive in fulfilling their own wants and desires regardless of the effect it has on other people.

When we draw our awareness to others, and away from ourselves we are reaching a higher level of consciousness, which benefits all of humankind. There is undeniable evidence to prove that when we accept each other as equals we experience peace in our world.

History has recorded numerous occasions of war and conflict due to one nation attempting to dominate another with their desire to be superior.

Many years ago, in Papua New Guinea, two tribes continued to fight against each other for several generations. Each generation fought and nursed their wounds only to fight again, killing and maiming more and more people. Finally, after years of struggle the two tribes realized that they must stop fighting or nothing would be left of their people, so the chiefs of the two tribes came together and brought with them a child they called the 'Peace Child'. This child, the son of one of the chiefs, was then adopted into the family of the opposing chief and while that child was alive the two chiefs promised to cease their fighting, because the adopted child had joined the two tribes together as a family.

This true story is a perfect example of how people can change their attitude and behaviour when the energy from within is used for the good of all.

I sometimes visualize millions of orange balloons being released into the sky all over the world on the same day to show our connection to each other as a symbolic gesture to heal us from our past sins. In Australia schools celebrate Harmony Day on the 19th. March and children are asked to wear orange clothing.

It's interesting to note that flags of war representing the armed forces rarely, if ever, have the colour orange in them.

If we believe in the possibility that we can all be related—through our great, great, great, great grandparents, then one of our relatives could have been instrumental in causing pain to another in the past and, for our future relatives, we need to keep the slate clean now. If we believe in reincarnation then we could have been, in a -past-life, one of those brutal, deceptive individuals who destroyed another persons' self-respect by enforcing our beliefs upon them. Collectively we are all accountable, and the only way we can eradicate this blemish from our own souls is to wisely connect with each other through sharing our love, time, talents, resources, whatever is available to us with each other now. But before we go global, we need to harmoniously connect to our own family and friends.

Jenny Lind was a world-famous opera singer who was known as the Swedish Nightingale. She thrilled thousands of people with her live performances, and then one day she left the stage and never returned. Years later, when asked why she had abandoned the stage at the height of her career, she said it was because her crowded schedule was robbing her of precious time with her family and friends. Her ultimate fulfilment came, not in career and money but in her relationship with family and friends. Jenny Lind had found her way to keep this chakra open.

When we use the energy from the Svadisthana chakra to support others we benefit too. Years ago, there was a popular song titled, 'With a little help from my friends'.

The words being - and the world will be a better place, for me, and you. This is so true because when we care and share with each other the world truly does become a better place to live in.

Geese can teach us a lot about helping and supporting one another. When they journey from North to South, they fly in a V formation to minimise the effort for the birds following the leaders. It also allows the flock to cover approximately a seventy-one percent greater flying range than if each bird flew on its own. If a goose falls out of formation it immediately feels the drag and resistance of trying to go it alone and quickly gets back into formation to take advantage of the lifting power of the birds up the front. Should the lead goose get tired he will rotate back in the wing and another goose takes over the lead role. The geese flying behind the leaders honk to encourage those up front to keep up their speed. And if a goose becomes ill, or is wounded by a shot, and falls out of formation, two other geese follow it down to help and protect it. They stay with the injured goose until it can fly again, or until it dies. Then only will they fly off on their own, or with another formation, until they catch up with their original group.

This chakra is all about giving, so we can experience exaltation of the soul. Recently a study was done at Warwick University on people who had won the lottery. The ones who gave using their wisdom from within reported increased happiness with their new wealthy status. Those who were mean reported no difference in their lives or stated that it had changed into a more negative lifestyle. The worst case was a man named Phil Kitchen who won 5 million dollars and then drank himself to death eighteen months later. Another man, Mark Gardiner, after winning thirty million dollars said his life was full of stress and aggravation. He also said that he had rejected all demands for his money. One woman who won $920,000 said it made no difference to her lifestyle at all. She was still working in her same job and had kept her win a complete secret from everyone. None of these people used their lucky win to make a positive difference to their lives or to the lives of others.

Then there was the story of Barbara and Ray Wragg who won twenty-one million dollars and immediately gave away two-thirds of their fortune. When interviewed Barbara said, "We are now even happier than we were before our win. We realized that we had much more than we could use, and that the best thing we could do with the rest was to use it to do a bit of good for others. That's why we decided to give the money away." This is how we respond when the orange chakra is activated through the divine energy, everyone becomes a winner—the people who won the lottery and the people who received.

During the festival of Diwali in India I was so impressed to see people passing on their boxes of special sweets to others. After eating some themselves and rather than saving them for the next day they gave them to others, who then passed it on after they had had some. This way everyone in their village or community had some sweets. In our western culture we tend to overeat rather than share.

During the Chinese New Year people *give* each other oranges and mandarins as a sign of friendship. The sharing of food is especially beneficial for the unblocking of this chakra.

In Hindi, Indian language, khana means food—the words Svadisthana sounds like khana, at the end, and this chakra is located near the stomach in our body. When we feed others physical food, we are feeding ourselves spiritual food, through the Divine source.

The third chakra's Sanskrit name is Manipura, and it is connected to our physical, mental and emotional power.

It is linked to the Sun and is represented by the colour yellow, the third colour in the rainbow. Just as the sun gives life, energy, to everything on earth so too does this chakra give energy to our body, in fact some of the body's parts such as the liver, gall bladder, intestines and stomach perform so well when this chakra is open, it even intensifies the power of the brain.

Recently, Australian scientists at the Queensland centre for schizophrenia research unearthed evidence of a link between sunshine and schizophrenia. The theory is that vitamin D deficiency during pregnancy, caused by a lack of sunlight, can alter the development of a child's brain in the womb. This causes the genes in the brain to become less active and the ventricles become enlarged, both linked to schizophrenia.

The Australian indigenous people have a yellow sun on their flag because it represents the life-force energy. In ancient beliefs people looked upon the sun as a god, and in Judaism and Christianity we are told that it was God's first creation. Because this energy centre is linked to personal power and radiance it is not surprising to find that the symbol for the Manipura chakra is the sun. Since ancient times, people have recognized that life on earth depended upon the sun. They visualized God as Light and Life, Power and Radiance and the Sun became a symbol for God, who is the centre of all creation because the planets revolve around the sun. This was the belief in ancient Hinduism. But the early Christians interpreted the Bible differently. They believed the earth was in the centre as God's creation and our dwelling-place. They also needed to draw attention away from the power of the sun god, so even after the Italian scientist, Galileo discovered that the earth moved around the sun and not vice versa the Christian authorities made him deny this claim or face torture. They were afraid that people would lose their faith if they knew that the earth was not the centre of the universe as they believed it said in the Bible.

Hindu mystics of ancient times during deep transcendental meditation awakened the energy from this chakra and described it as a radiant force of the sacred fire; and so, the Manipura chakra became known as the personal fire, likened to the power of the sun.

Through our modern technology, we know that the most powerful object in our solar system is the Sun. The temperature at its core is 15,000,000 degrees centigrade and we feel the heat at 30 degrees centigrade!

The pressure that builds up from this heat at the core of the Sun takes a million years to reach its surface—and then that heat travels 150 million kilometres to Earth and we can still feel it. Five million tons of pure energy is released from the sun every second. Even without all this information the mystics of old knew the immense power of the sun. They also knew that when they used the energy from this chakra, they could accomplish amazing feats without suffering physical or mental fatigue, in the same way that the sun keeps burning with its endless source of energy. They kept their bodies and minds active using this inner source of energy, and believed it was from this chakra that we developed the strong drive and motivation to go forward in life. It was seen as the vital force behind our successes in life, which allowed us to transcend beyond the bounds of our humanness. In other words, we could do and achieve tasks that our human mind could never have perceived.

This quote from Winston Churchill tells us how to use this power: "The only guide to man is his conscience, the only shield to his memory is the rectitude and sincerity of his actions. It is very imprudent to walk through life with this shield as we are often mocked by the failure of our hopes and the upsetting of our calculations. With this shield however the fates may play with us we march always in the ranks of honour.

Success is going from failure to failure without losing your enthusiasm."

When this chakra is unblocked, we have the courage to go forward. We can relinquish the past, live energetically in the present, and have great hopes for the future. The energy from this yellow chakra gives us radiance, like the sun; we glow from within, and it is expressed by a positive attitude in all we do.

Mother Teresa of Calcutta displayed this inner power in a very humble manner. Once, when a reporter commented about all the great 'deeds' she had done she replied, "Oh they were just little deeds, done with great love."

When Mother Teresa first started out on her missionary work with her God-given dream of helping the sick and orphaned children of Calcutta, she had no financial resources.

So, she and a couple of her faithful sisters decided to go begging. Letters to wealthy businesses seeking aid had received no response. Hoping the personal approach might work she sought out her first donor with her hand humbly stretched out and the man spat into her hand whilst she was still asking him to help her financially support orphaned children. Without any change in the tone of her voice she gently withdrew that hand and putting her other hand out she said, "That was for me, now this hand is for the children." The man was so taken aback that from that moment on he became one of her biggest financial supporters.

Mother Teresa used her power, and whatever resources she had including the money she received as part of the Nobel Peace Prize to help others. Her needs were secondary to the needs of others. She would take sick and dying people off the streets of Calcutta and care for them. It was an act of caring never to dominate or control. No one had to convert to her beliefs or to conform to her way of living. She said that everyone had free will which was a gift from God and that each person had to decide for themselves what was best for them.

Some religious people begin with acts of kindness and then they dominate and indoctrinated those people who are most vulnerable. When power is used to control it is not from the divine source.

The great Indian leader Mahatma Gandhi also had this personal power and expressed aptly the difference between using it for the good of humankind, or for the heinous destruction of the weak and innocent. He said: "the things that will destroy us are – politics without principle; pleasure without conscience; wealth without work; knowledge without character; business without morality; science without humanity; and worship without sacrifice."

Oprah Winfrey, the American television talk-show hostess has used her personal power to help millions of people through her television shows. Her work has literally saved many people's lives—all this from a black woman who was not born with the proverbial silver spoon in her mouth. The energy from this chakra allows her to share her wealth generously with others.

And Princess Diana during her short lifetime used this power to help many who were born less fortunate than her.

The most amazing thing is that this power is available to all of us when we tap into the energy of this chakra.

Many years ago, in Jodhpur India there lived a young man named Amit who felt deep within him the need to live a spiritual life teaching about God. He shunned the idea of an arranged marriage, so he left home, put on a saffron robe, and sat on the banks of the Ganges River living the life of an ascetic. His thoughts often led him to the notion of making money—"If

I set up an ashram and inspired people with my thoughts, I could become very successful." But after a few months of donning his saffron clothes and sitting on the banks of the Ganga he became very depressed and frustrated, because nothing changed, no one appeared eager to listen to him. He returned home disappointed. Then one day, by chance, he heard that a great sadhu was visiting a nearby town, so he saved up his money and went to hear this great preacher.

With thousands of other people, he listened with rapt attention at the words that flowed from the mouth of the sadhu. To Amit it was as if a Divine force was speaking, and the listeners were all hypnotized. He visualized himself as a great preacher, speaking eloquently for hours on end and people listening to him with rapt attention. He stayed in that town for several days, each day hoping he could personally speak to the great sadhu, he felt so sincere in his endeavour to serve God. Then his opportunity came early one morning when he saw the sadhu sitting in the dawn light on the river-bank reading a holy book. He approached the sadhu cautiously and with his hands in a prayer position he bowed respectfully in front of him. The sadhu looked at Amit for a moment and, without responding, started reading his book again. Amit waited for half an hour. The sadhu looked at him again, but this time he spoke to him and said, "Until you shed hypocrisy you will not be able to achieve anything. You wish to be accepted as a great sadhu when you are hypocritical and immoral." Amit knew now how great the power of the sadhu was because he knew his innermost thoughts without Amit saying one word.

For the next few weeks Amit took every opportunity he could to be of some service to the sadhu, whether it was to get him a drink of water or dust the grass off his shawl; and he listened carefully to everything he preached.

Several days later the sadhu spoke to him again, he told Amit he had to reverently meditate and pray and fast for one month and he explained to Amit the process of the sadhana—sacred ritual. "Start on the fifth day of the lunar month, wake-up early and, after taking a bath in the river, put on only a yellow dhoti. Then sit on a mat that is yellow in colour. You must sit in a padmasana posture with your eyes steady and back straight. Hold a rosary of sixty-four coral beads in one hand and a green twig of a banyan tree in the other hand. Counting the beads recite this mantra twenty-one times. Fifty-four repetitions of the mantra will make one round of the beads. Continue with the recitation of the mantra for thirty days. Start before sunbreak and repeat this at noon and at sunset. Do not use any intoxicants during this time and of course your little intake of food must be vegetarian. During your sadhana there must be no feeling of laziness or listlessness and do not talk to any man or woman."

On the fifth day of the lunar-month he started his sadhana. After he completed it, he went to a large ashram and requested the director to use him as a guest speaker. After a bit of hesitation, because the director had never heard Amit speak before, he agreed to let Amit speak that evening. When Amit took his place on the stage that evening his heart was beating fast, there was a huge crowd in front of him. After silently saying a short mantra, he felt energised, and he began to speak. There was pin-drop silence as the audience listened with rapt attention, and when he concluded his talk, after an hour and twenty minutes, the crowd applauded loudly, which was against the normal tradition in the Ashram. Amit was amazed at himself because he had no idea of what he spoke or how he spoke. The director invited him to be their speaker for a month and tape-recorded his speeches for future use.

Amit went on to open his own Ashram to which thousands of people came and even though he was financially well off he was never consciously aware of it because he had lost all interest in material things. For Amit, the energy from the Manipura chakra enabled him to fulfil his ambition of helping others through teaching and preaching.

It is important to have a purpose in your life. What is it that you could be doing but are not?

Work at fulfilling your cherished dreams and use the energy from this chakra to accomplish them. Do not fall into the trap of blaming someone else when you are not reaching your full potential.

Like this Christian joke, 'Adam blamed Eve, Eve blamed the Serpent, and the Serpent never had a leg to stand on.' Blame is just 'passing the buck' and gets us nowhere.

On a trip into the country town of Wagin I heard about a young man whose tractor had rolled over pinning him between the seat and the road. His face was pushed into the side of his fatally injured dog, he had a broken knee, and he was barely breathing. One shoulder was against the tractor the other was on the road. The young man said, "I had to decide whether

I was going to die or get out." With a desperate push, using all the energy from within his body, he got his head out and then lay there unconscious. The force he used to free himself was so intense it broke his collarbone. A worker found him walking around in a daze. Today he is well and getting on with his life.

Personal power comes to us in so many ways. My mother in her late seventies was a chronic asthmatic constantly ill then my father got cancer and she was able to care for him right up to the time of his death. Where did the strength come from? I believe it was from within.

I read about Quentin Kenihan, a young man who spends his life in a wheelchair because he has a brittle bone disease and his limbs do not grow. He said, "I think in life we all have to use what we have to our advantage. Being in a wheelchair has been a detriment to me in so many ways, but it can also be a bonus because it's difficult for people to say no to disabled people." He has his own production company producing documentaries and short films.

Even though he lacks physical power he uses his tremendous inner power.

When the Manipura chakra is open every achievement we accomplish, that we thought we could never achieve gives us a feeling of personal pride, not the show-off pride, but an expanded positive self-image. We must all strive to reach our highest potential, and we can achieve this by using the power that is within us. When we acknowledge and share our achievements with others our confidence gives others confidence too.

Jesus, the great master, told his followers, "Let your light shine before men, so that they may see your good works." When we shine others shine too, it is contagious. And as we are liberated from our own fears our newfound willpower and air of confidence automatically liberates others from their own fears of inadequacy.

One of the greatest writers of poetry, W.B. Yeats wrote about unimagined power of the individual mind and body in his poems.

I believe the power he referred to is the energy of this chakra. This biological phenomenon, accountable only by each person's experiences is often regarded with suspicion and disbelief by the same people who will readily accept extraordinary instinctive behaviour in lower forms of life. Take for example the spider, the smallest of which is the size of a full-stop less than half a millimetre, yet they all build incredible webs by instinct.

A spiderling has no trouble building its first web from silk which comes from its spinnerets. This spider silk is amazing. It is thin and light, almost invisible yet incredibly flexible and tough, as strong as steel wire of the same size. Some spiders can make thirty-three metres of silk in one day from which they build some spectacular webs.

With our technology of today scientists have transplanted genes from a spider into cells from a cow and hamster to make those cells produce the protein that makes spider silk. This step could point the way to commercial production of the tough fibre, long admired for its strength and durability. Spider silk is more resistant than Kevlar, stronger than iron, and is biodegradable. Researchers say the silk, if produced commercially, could be used for products from surgical thread to soft body armour for burn victims.

In the same vein, what incredible possibilities can be attributed to this chakra's powerful energy once conclusive evidence of its existence can be furnished?

The fact that highly intelligent minds have not been able to give any recognition to this extremely subtle, life-force energy does not validate its non-existence. We still have a long way to go before we can come to any complete realization of the human body, especially the human brain, which is still in a continuous evolutionary process towards a higher form of consciousness. For those who wish to pursue their consciousness beyond the normal limits they can achieve this through meditation; and then this spiritual energy will transform them mentally and physically; even to the extent of keeping their bodies free from disease and illness.

An Ayurveda practitioner told me that if this Manipura chakra was unblocked, we would never get Diabetes; he was referring to adult diabetes.

This concludes the three lower energy centres –

Muladhara: red; our connection to earth since its conception.

> Psalms 139: "when I was being made in secret, intricately wrought in the depths of the earth, you knew me."

Svadisthana orange, is our connection to each other—love thy neighbour is the goal we must all seek.

Manipura, yellow, is the development of our identity and personal power and helps us to reach our highest potential.

The energy centre in the middle of the seven major chakras is the heart chakra called Anahata the aim here is to achieve a pure heart.

"Blessed are the pure in heart, for they shall see God" were the words spoken by Jesus to his Christian followers.

Today Roman Catholics say prayers to the Sacred Heart of Jesus using a picture of Jesus showing rays of light radiating from his heart.

Roman Catholic Christians use the image of the Sacred Heart of Jesus to further enhance their spirituality, and they recite prayers (similar to mantras) to the Sacred Heart of Jesus. This image usually depicts rays of light emitting from the heart of Jesus.

This chakra is represented by the colour green, the next colour in the rainbow.

Sadhus linked this colour green to plants and saw chlorophyll, the green in leaves that keeps plants alive, in the same vein as plasma in the heart keeps our bodies alive.

And just as the heart supplies blood to the whole body, the leaves make and send enriched food to the whole plant in an amazing process called photosynthesis. The similarity in which the leaf and heart function is astounding. Both require air to function, and both distribute the food through veins. The functions of both are way beyond what any human mind could invent—the average heart pumps 7,200 litres of blood per day and just one hectare of corn can supply 325 people with their total oxygen supply for the day. The study of photosynthesis in plants began in 1771, but the connection between this heart chakra and the plant was made thousands of years ago through inner wisdom that has always been available to us long before things could be scientifically proven. Some people refer to it as inspiration, those things that come to us through the super-conscious mind.

Ancient Egyptians were aware of this power-centre of the heart. When the embalmers mummified the Pharaohs' body after death, they removed all the body parts; stomach, liver, lungs, intestines, including the brain which they pulled out of the nose with a large hook, and placed them into special containers called canopic jars. Only the heart was left in the body because they believed it was the centre of all life—even the one after death.

Today Scientists say that thinking with your heart, and the heart being the symbol of love, are no longer metaphoric but literal. They, along with neuro-cardiologists have found the heart to be an important neuro-endocrine gland, as it produces and releases Atrial Natriuretic Factor which has an important effect on every operation in the limbic system. Sixty-five per cent of the heart cells are neural cells that function in a similar way to the brain.

Does this mean that our heart stores memories in the same way the brain does?

The expression,' to put your heart and soul into something,' and to learn something, 'by heart,' were not idle expressions after all!

Yogis knew our heart thinks and feels, thousands of years ago. Now science is proving it and telling us that the heart is the centre of an electro-magnetic field that can be traced even 10-12 feet away from the body.

The energy from this chakra purifies the lungs and assists them in functioning to capacity.

If you look at the diagram you will understand why the energy from this heart chakra works so well on the lungs too.

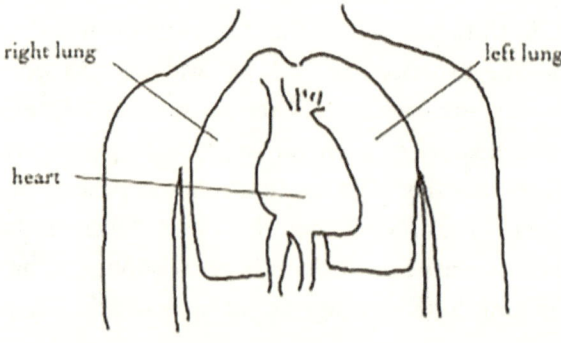

Yogis have developed simple breathing exercises to activate the energy from this chakra, without putting any strain on other parts of the body, as happens when running or jogging.

Try this exercise to strengthen the heart. Place your hands in two fists upon your shoulders.

Take a deep breath in and shoot your arms with clenched fists straight up. Then as you let the breath out forcefully bring your hands down. Repeat this action twenty times.

To get the maximum benefit from this exercise do it outdoors near a tree, that way you know that your intake of oxygen is fresh.

Because the Anahata chakra stands for unconditional love it is a hard chakra to keep unblocked. As human beings we have a natural tendency to love conditionally, but when we unblock this chakra, we will get a glimpse of the divine love, which is eternal and totally forgiving and then we will express unconditional love.

Many years ago, while I was absorbed in deep meditation, I experienced such exquisite love, to which I have never found anything parallel on this earthly planet. As I sank deeper and deeper within, I felt my consciousness grow, extending from my normal state my mind expanded as if there were no barriers, no limitations, between the conscious state and the super conscious state. The vision in front of me was that of a young man, whom I instantly perceived was my body, holding the hand of a beautiful little girl who was obviously my child. The moment she looked up at me I was intensely aware of a feeling of love so profound it left me entranced and in awe—totally inconceivable by the conscious mind. It was as if a marvellous expansion was penetrating the very depths of my being in the location of the Anahata chakra. When I returned to normal consciousness I was struck by the beauty and depth of that love, an experience beyond all and everything belonging to this world.

I spoke about this to a psychic acquaintance of mine and asked why I did not feel the same love for my sons, who are everything I ever wished for in this life. She told me it was because I love here as a human being whilst the other was an experience of spiritual love, which is unconditional love at a higher consciousness.

The energy from the Anahata chakra allows us to experience unconditional love that is deeply embedded in us and is part of a person's personality from birth. This manner of loving is not something that is learnt or developed, but instead it is an acutely conscious aspect from within, which, when nurtured in the proper environment intensifies to greater heights.

It is my firm belief that all people on earth have the capacity to give and receive love through the energy of the Anahata chakra, regardless of their earthly experiences. Because even though some meet more opposition than support in their early lives they still manage to love unconditionally and keep this chakra open.

This is how it was for a young man in Calcutta who had started life on the streets, abandoned at birth and cared for in an inconsistent way by other street people but who had love pouring out of him, despite his unloved and neglected childhood. It all began when he found a stray puppy who loved him with complete abandonment. From the moment they met they shared everything. Through this puppy he discovered he had a natural affinity with animals and, one day, without any hassles, he saved a runaway buffalo for a stranger and thereby landed his first job in a nearby village caring for a herd of buffaloes.

That is how I met him, while driving through the village I stopped to look at the buffaloes, especially a white one, and he came up to me and told me all about the herd with great affection. He had given them all names, and he said each had its own personality, and he pointed out the weak one that had been timid, that was now strong and could work as hard as any of the others. He was married to a shy smiling village girl. He called her over to meet me. She came slowly, hiding most of her face with her sari and all his children raced over to me. Without any firmness, in his voice he kept telling them "Hutto, Hutto, Hutto, go away, do not bother our visitor."

I could see the love in him for his family, it was then that I realised he must have been born with an incredible amount of love within him, that the puppy had brought to fruition.

The caring and sharing we give to a pet helps to increase our capacity to love and for unblocking this chakra, but it must not become an obsessive, inclusive love for the pet, that excludes human love and interaction. Our priority is to love human beings unconditionally because we are all created in the same image as the Divine source of all creation. If the love for a pet is so consuming that it excludes all others, then this possessive, unbalanced love will block this Anahata chakra, which will then lead to serious ramifications for all the other major chakras, and can cause ill health, especially stomach and bowel complaints.

Our focus must always be people, and then the energy from this chakra will keep us, 'full of life, which is the role of the heart; and we will have no difficulty loving others with an open heart. It will never occur to us that we are 'better' than anyone else, only when this chakra is blocked does pride and prejudice fill our lives; and then we develop a tendency to put others down to try to lift ourselves up.

The energy from this Anahata chakra enables us to lift the spirit of others and then we feel uplifted too.

Throughout the ages people have expressed love, promoted love, and some have even been prepared to die for love. We even have a special day for love called Valentine's Day that goes back to the time of the Roman Empire.

At that time, the emperor was more interested in his army, than in family life and was convinced that single men made better soldiers than married ones, so he made a law banning marriage.

Saint Valentine, a Catholic monk defied the emperor and married young couples in secret.

There was another Saint Valentine who also lived under Roman rule. He led a simple life working with the poor people and orphaned children to whom he took the message of God's love. Some Romans did not like his beliefs and the message he was spreading so they had him imprisoned. The poor people and orphaned children were so upset they wrote notes of love and comfort and threw them to him through his cell window. Valentine's Day was named after these two saints, who both practiced giving love, even in the face of adversity.

Moses, the great prophet from the Hebrew texts told the Israelite people "You shall love your neighbour as yourself and any stranger who sojourns with you shall be to you as the native among you, and you shall love him as yourself." (Leviticus 19:18b, 34)

This emphasises the importance of loving all of mankind, not just love the people in our immediate family or group but reach out to strangers with the same compassion and acknowledgement.

The great English writer William Shakespeare from the 16th century focused many of his plays around the theme of love. In Romeo and Juliet,

Shakespeare's greatest love story, he describes love as a brilliant light, and when Romeo sees Juliet, for the first time, Shakespeare writes it as an aura of light around Juliet and Romeo calls her an angel, "Oh, speak again bright angel."

And then Romeo says, "The brightness of her cheek would shame those stars, as daylight doth a lamp."

Shakespeare writes about their feelings of love as a bright and comforting light. When this great love is denied Romeo and Juliet, Shakespeare's descriptive writings go from brilliant light to darkness:

It was the lark, the herald of the morn,
Do lace the severing clouds in yonder east.
Stands tiptoe on the misty mountain tops.
I must be gone and live or stay and die.

Here the absence of love brings darkness, it goes from lighter and lighter to darker and darker our woes and finally to, 'The sun for sorrow will not show his head'.

People talk about a 'broken heart or a 'heavy heart'. We all know that the heart has not physically broken down or got heavier, but what has happened is that the energy from this chakra has been restricted, and life becomes a burden.

Jesus told his followers, "The sorrow in my heart is so great that it almost crushes me" (1Matt.26).

To recharge this energy centre after a 'broken heart' one needs to move on and love again. It does not have to be to any one person—just giving and receiving love keeps this chakra flowing freely, because there is an endless supply of love within us.

Even when we lose someone to physical death, we must not swap, living our life loving one another for living a life of grief and sorrow.

Yogis tell us that the heart holds memories and now people like Paul Pearsall, who works with Psychoneuroimmunology, is proving this theory with the research he is doing with heart-transplant recipients. According to him the heart, has the ability, to retain and transmit information and emotions.

One story to add weight to this theory is that of an eight-year-old girl who received a donor heart and soon afterwards began to have dreadful nightmares of being murdered. From a quiet, loving child she became a child gripped by fear. At first her parents thought it was the after-effects of the operation, but after several sessions with a psychiatrist they realized it was more than that, so, following his advice they asked for more information about the child who was the heart donor, which had not been given to her parents due to the privacy laws. After some hesitation by the medical staff, they were told that the donor heart came from a young girl who had been murdered. The parents then contacted the police and gave them all the information their daughter had given them during her nightmares. They were so detailed, the police were able to find the murderer, who confessed to committing the crime. Everything the heart transplant patient reported was completely accurate, and the only way she could have obtained so much information was via the heart.

Cemeteries tell some beautiful stories of deep human love. In Melbourne's Kew cemetery there is a special tomb that tells such a story. The tomb is placed on its own in a lovely garden surrounded by a wall with large ornate gates. On entering one sees a magnificent large rotunda made from Italian marble with tall carved pillars. Inside the rotunda is a life-size replica of a beautiful woman lying on a coffin, watched over by an angel, with messages of love carved into every part of the monument, from the high-domed ceiling to the floor and walls.

The story goes that a wealthy woman married her much younger gardener. Everyone believed he had married her for her money, but when his adored wife died a year later in childbirth, he spent her entire fortune, that he had inherited, on this magnificent monument as proof of his sincerity and love.

The magnificent building, 'The Taj Mahal' in India was built by Shah Jahan in 1632 in memory of his beloved wife, Mumtaz Mahal.

Shah Jahan said that he had everything life could offer, but it all paled in significance when compared to his love for Mumtaz Mahal.

After her death he spent the next 15 years building this huge mausoleum of pure white marble, 580 x 304 metres in size with the central dome rising to a height of 33 metres. The front archway and sides were engraved with beautiful intricate patterns and adorned with precious and semi-precious stones, and an exquisite, filigreed marble screen, studded with precious stones, was built around the marble tomb.

He called her - the light of his life, and the reflection of light on the Taj Mahal is amazing, from every angle and approach the subtle changes of light on its opalescent marble surface reflects indescribable beauty.

The Shah was so consumed by his grief, after Mumtaz Mahals' death, he was unaware of his son's rebellion until it was too late. Prince Aurangzeb's army defeated the Shah's army, and the prince had his father imprisoned. The Shah's only request was for a window to be made in his cell facing the Taj Mahal, so he could gaze upon the tomb of his beloved wife. The Shah lived in this cell for eight years.

Stories told about him by people who attended to him during the years said his great love for Mumtaz Mahal sustained him in such a way he was able to live out his remaining days in peace without any bitterness or hatred.

To live in peace is one of the blessings of the radiant energy from the Anahata chakra, which is recharged continuously by the divine energy.

These stories of deep love and devotion were from the heart with love continuing even after death. Sadly, some people consider spending large sums of money on tombstones rather wasteful, but nothing done out of love is ever wasted.

When something is done out of pure love the benefits are forever, as in the beauty of the Taj Mahal which is visited by millions of tourists each year.

When meditating on the heart chakra, say this affirmation to bring healing to the heart.

From my heart I release all pain, anxiety, illness, and negativity.

Into my heart I restore complete wellness.

Or you can say this prayer before meditating, to open-up this heart chakra.

May the words of my mouth,
and the meditation of my heart
be always acceptable to you God,
my strength, and my redeemer.

When I came to Australia almost fifty years ago it was difficult for me because I was a dark-skinned immigrant from India. At that time, it seemed as if everyone was prejudiced against everyone else with a kind of invisible hierarchy scale for immigrants.

It started with Italians and Greeks, then Chinese and Indians. I understood my future Australian mother-in-law's feelings of resentment towards me the first time we met. It did not take long for us to get close though, without the least bit of prejudice between us.

The common bond of love, because we both loved the same person, took all prejudice away.

It is a sad fact that within the Christian faith, which preaches love as its main ingredient, we see exhibited some of the most heightened forms of prejudice and bigotry amongst its fellow Christians.

Wasn't the Church of England better than the Roman Catholic Church and vice-versa?

When we work with the energy from the heart Chakra, we do not harbour thoughts like these, we see all people as equal. This is love at a spiritual level. When we learn to practice true love, we learn how to forgive and release all grudges and resentments. Unconditional love and forgiveness are one and the same and the energy from this centre helps us to walk that path.

Some years ago, relatives of friends of mine, a mother and father, came home from work to find that their eldest son had, in a fit of temper, killed their youngest son.

The priest at the little boy's funeral said,

"I don't even pretend to understand why such a horrific tragedy should have occurred. But we have to continue living."

For this family to continue living after this horrendous tragedy will be difficult. With love and support from others they will learn to have faith in themselves and with the energy from the heart chakra they can even accomplish the impossible and learn to forgive their eldest son. When we give ourselves permission to forgive, we are making the choice to move forward on our journey of life, and this leads to happiness. The sad loss of this family's little boy will remain with them forever, but the bitterness will go creating within them a more compassionate nature.

Buddhists believe that to reach a blissful state of contentment we must let go of all desires because it is our desires that keep us in a continuous state of wanting because as soon as we get what we want, we desire something else. The novelty of the new item wears off quickly when it is a want and not a need. Often our desires are created through envy. The saying, green with envy, is when we desire things others have, this creates feelings of jealousy within us, which then blocks this green chakra and our capacity to love, because jealousy is a type of fear, and fear is the opposite of love.

In the Bible, the tenth commandment 'Thou shalt not covet', meaning wanting something that belongs to someone else, was taught to the people of Israel as an act of sinfulness, to be avoided at all costs. Desiring material things, which is coveting in this commandment, creates in our mind uneasiness and restlessness.

To keep this green chakra open we need to count our blessings, however simple they may be, and remain optimistic in all situations.

Practise adding one thing every day to your blessings list and watch it grow, this will eradicate all feelings of envy and a distinct feeling of contentment will prevail. This wanting is in the mind—once we focus on our needs and not our wants this continuous wanting will stop and we will be happier. So many people lead stressful lives today working so hard to provide for their family's wants, that they eventually end up believing they need, because everyone attaches so much importance to material things.

As parents we need to be very selective when buying things for our children. From a young age teach children how to differentiate between a want and a need. And even if it is a need, make them wait for it—patience is truly a virtue, and then upon reflection the child might not want it anymore. Children who learn to identify needs from wants, and those who develop patience, are more loving and unselfish than those children who think that every want is a need and that their wants must be had immediately.

Tulsidas said, "Real happiness of heart cannot be attained without giving up the idea of I, and mine.

Mahatma Gandhi said, "Earth has enough for everyone's needs but not for everyone's greed." Children need to understand that greed affects not just themselves but all of mankind.

This story from Aesop's Fables, they were based on ancient Buddhist stories, is a good one to read and discuss with children.

One day a dog was racing off with a big bone in his mouth. On his way home he had to walk across a bridge over a stream. As he was running across the bridge he glanced into the water and much to his surprise he saw another dog that also had a bone in his mouth. The dog stopped and thought, "If I can scare that dog off, I can grab his bone and then I can have two." So, he snarled at the other dog baring his teeth and as he made a deep growl, he dropped the bone from his mouth into the stream.

Greed and selfishness go together.

The energy from this green chakra helps us to give unconditionally and our personality becomes totally unselfish. When giving makes us feel happy it is coming from our heart. On the other hand, when giving makes us feel uncomfortable it is coming from a selfish personality, one that is either genetic, and/or conditioned through unhappy experiences.

The energy from this chakra will allow a transformation to occur within the selfish person's personality so that giving will come naturally without the mind setting up barriers to sabotage them from giving.

The expression, 'He's/she's all heart' implies a very generous soul, one that has evolved to a higher level of spirituality through the opening of the heart chakra.

The golden rule for this chakra is that we must give to receive. People usually associate giving with time and money and servitude. These are all excellent ways of giving but always keep in mind that this chakra calls us to be givers of love.

This is how St. Paul explained love to the early Christians.

Love is patient and kind,
Love is not jealous or boastful,

It is not arrogant or rude,
Love does not insist on its own way,
It does not rejoice in wrong but rejoices in the right,
Love never ends.

This type of love flows from the energy of the Anahata chakra. It is love in its fullest, our human love combined with the Divine love. It allows us to abandon all negative thoughts of hatred, jealousy and revenge that are all manifestations of our own creation. Hindus call it atmik, self-inflicted. When the heart chakra is blocked, we harbour these negative feelings and the longer these feelings of hatred and jealousy stay locked in the heart the more they will intensify. If after a time they are not released, they will cause mental and health problems, with some becoming so deranged they resort to taking the lives of their own children and themselves.

The early philosophers of Hinduism and yoga around 700BC said that the answer to all human problems was Samyakjnana—proper knowledge. They believed that it was the absence of Samyakjnana that caused dukkha (sorrow); in western culture it is the broken-heart syndrome, which is often caused when relationships fail due to an inability to communicate sensibly.

The energy from this chakra controls the emotions at a high level of sensibility and this power of Self-control will bring about emotional and mental equilibrium.

Dukkha will then be replaced by Purusha, harmony of body, mind, and soul.

In Patanjali's' Yoga Sutras, 300BC, the harmonious relationship between the body and the mind is through the energy of this chakra, which is activated through Dharana, concentration, Dhyana, meditation, and this leads to Samadhi, enlightenment.

When love flows through the Anahata chakra we maintain excellent health, because this inner energy acts as both a curative and as a preventive measure against illness, especially with mental health problems which is usually the cause of emotional trauma.

Keep the Anahata chakra open and you will love yourself with your whole heart and you will love your neighbour as yourself and then what a wonderful world this will be.

The fifth energy centre, Vishuddha, is located near the throat and is represented by the colour blue. When the energy from this chakra is flowing freely it works to physically strengthen the ears, nose, and throat. It is the breath of life both physically and spiritually.

The Vishuddha chakra is linked to the lower chakras through the heart chakra, which is located near the lungs, so the air carried through the throat to the lungs works systematically with both these chakras.

If we stay focused on the rhythm of the breath, we will consciously be aware of the Vishuddha chakra. During a busy day make it your business to stop and reflect on the breath; listen to it, feel it, and be grateful for your nose, throat and lungs and then common colds and sore throats will not be so common anymore.

The energy from this chakra also enhances the physical and spiritual functioning of listening and speaking. Its Sanskrit name gave Buddha his title because he spoke words of spiritual wisdom to his followers.

When the Vishuddha chakra is open our speech has more clarity to it, because we speak with greater confidence.

Years ago, I remember listening to Joni Erickson Tada, a disabled young woman, speak on television and I was amazed at her natural confidence. She had been in a diving accident which had left her totally paralysed from the neck down. Yet there she was on T.V. totally poised, answering questions, and talking confidently. Later she said that when she had been asked to come onto the show—"My heart was in my throat," and she did not think she would have had the confidence to speak on national television. She said she drew on her inner strength and that is how she got her confidence; though later she said, "I don't recall all I said."

This last statement is an example of the super-conscious mind at work—when someone speaks powerful words that inspire others, and they cannot recall those words, it is coming from the energy of the throat chakra.

The energy from this chakra gives us the ability to speak freely. It stops us from, holding things back, and allows us to, speak our mind, even when we feel threatened by doing so.

Adults, especially parents, who do not 'speak out' against those whom they know are physically or sexually abusing children, do so out of fear, which manifests itself when this chakra is blocked. Deep in their heart they want to speak out, but they cannot.

A woman I know was beaten by her father throughout her childhood and teenage years while her stepmother stood back silently and allowed it to happen.

One day as an adult she boarded a plane and paid her father a surprise visit and she was able to say all the words she had never been able to say before. Her father listened to it all silently and even though it did not improve the relationship between them, she felt as if a huge burden had been lifted from her shoulders. She said, "I felt such a release letting out all the things I'd bottled up over the years."

When the Vishuddha chakra is un-blocked we cannot bottle things up in our throat. We say those things that need to be said with wisdom and confidence whenever it is necessary to do so. This freedom of speech stops bitterness and hate from festering within, which is harmful to our wellbeing. In life we all need to stand up to a bully, like this woman's father. When we do that, they will quickly back down because a bully is an insecure person living in fear, not love, and the energy from within will give us the strength to do it.

I always admire people who speak out against the injustices in this world.

Martin Luther King spoke out about the injustices that were being committed to the black American people by the white Americans, and even when his life was at risk he continued to do so. He was against violence, so instead told people to pursue justice with the 'toughness of the serpent and the softness of the dove', which he interpreted as a tough mind and a tender heart.

His speeches did much to bridge the gap between the disadvantaged black people and the greedy, insensitive white people of America.

He said, "I believe that what self-centred men have torn down, other-centred men can build up." Martin Luther King knew about the spiritual centres that are within us. He also knew that fear had blocked this power for the black people, and he wanted them to release it, and be free.

The Burmese democratic resistance leader, Aung San Suu Kyi was put under house arrest for 11 years for speaking out against the military dictatorship in her country. Yet she still makes speeches, illegally, against the military government on behalf of the poor people in her country. Those that are illiterate, have no health care facilities and those who earn less than a dollar a day. People in her country are tortured and given lengthy prison sentences for the simplest of offences and children are used as slave labour for construction projects. Each time she makes a speech she puts her own life at risk. I heard her speak on radio once and when she was asked if she was ever frightened her answer was, "You cannot really be frightened of people you do not hate. Hate and fear go hand in hand."

In 1991 San Suu Kyi won the Noble Peace Prize but she was unable to receive it personally due to her house arrest. She says that her deep Buddhist faith has helped her to cope with her life of torture and confinement. She meditates daily, which she attributes to the soundness of her mental state. Even when her physical health suffered, almost to the point of death, she remained mentally strong and said, "But they never got me up here," meaning her head.

When we keep all the chakras open, we cannot be mentally broken no matter how stressful or difficult the situation. All the great leaders who spoke out against tyranny and injustice, Mahatma Gandhi, Nelson Mandela, Martin Luther King remained mentally alert in all situations because they used the strength from within. The energy from the Vishuddha chakra replaces hate with love and forgiveness.

Speaking out against wrong doings opens this chakra.

Some years ago, people we know, Chris and John were on holiday in London. They were sitting on a bus with their baggage near their feet and they could hear two people talking behind them. "I'm going to tell them." "No leave it. It has got nothing to do with you." "But I saw them do it. I feel I must tell them."

And with that the young lady tapped John on the shoulder and said, "Excuse me, but the young lad at the back of the bus has just taken your camera." John looked down at his bags and sure enough, the camera was missing. So, he called out to the young lads at the back of the bus and said, "Whoever has taken my camera I'd like it back, please."

Surprisingly, the lad who had taken it walked up to him and returned the camera.

When we, stick our neck out, as the young woman did, we are using the energy from the throat (neck) chakra. In this incident three people benefited due to one person's moral conscience. John got his camera back with the film of photos he could never replace, and the young lad got the opportunity to make a wrong right and the young lady would have felt good knowing that she had helped someone.

Yes, there is risk involved when we stick our necks out, but once we learn to speak out over the little things, bigger issues become easier to handle and as we build up confidence our character becomes stronger too.

All the religious leaders and prophets spoke out before establishing their new faith.

Jesus, the leader of the Christians was renowned for rebuking the hypocritical behaviour of some of the Jewish hierarchy. The dictionary gives the meaning for rebuked as a stern scolding. In other words, Jesus promoted firmness more than gentleness on certain issues.

By displaying our strong convictions, we are sending a firm message to others that we will not tolerate things that are detrimental to our physical, emotional, or spiritual well-being, and then our strength will give others strength to do the same.

Have you ever noticed how at a concert or any public gathering when one person stands up to applaud, a few more get up, till finally everyone is standing up applauding loudly?

Native Americans wore blue turquoise pendants near their throats to act as an energy booster for the Vishuddha chakra. Wear a blue turquoise necklace if you need help in speaking up, because crystal healers believe that this gemstone can get rid of, the lump in our throat.

When we speak freely, we feel venerated, our self-respect and self-esteem grow when we deal with troublesome issues wisely and considerately.

This is a Hindu story about one man who lost his soul and then found it again when he verbally released his pain, through the spoken word, using the energy from the Vishuddha chakra. Raicharan was a servant who attended to his master's needs diligently, from the time he started school, through college, and after he entered the judicial service.

Raicharan, who had no children of his own, devoted his life to Anukul his master, and paid only brief visits to his wife and elderly parents who lived nearby in a village.

In time, Anukul got married and his young wife took over charge of his household. At first Raicharan felt antagonistic towards her, but before the end of the first year all feelings of resentment disappeared when a new baby arrived.

Raicharan devoted his time to the care of the baby, and constantly praised the child to his mother, who also adored him. When the baby took his first faltering steps, Raicharan was there for him, and his joy knew no bounds when he began to call him Channa.

His father, Anukul showered him with gifts, even getting him a fine cart to sit in from Calcutta. One day, just after the monsoons, Raicharan was taking the little one for a walk, sitting in his cart, along the banks of the river when suddenly the child spotted a beautiful flower in a thorny bush. He pointed at it, and implored Channa with his huge black eyes to get it for him. So Raicharan moved over to the bush, to get the beautiful yellow flower for the child. It turned out to be a bit harder to retrieve than he had anticipated, but within a couple of minutes he had it in his grasp and with a tight pull it broke off into his hand. He stepped around the bush to hand it to his little master, but the child was gone.

In that first terrible moment his blood froze within him and the whole universe seemed to swim around him like a dark mist. With utter despair he started calling out, "Master, Master, little master." Raicharan ran back to the thorny bush, the cart nearby was still empty.

He ran frantically up and down the banks of the swollen river. But he saw nothing, except the water swiftly rushing by. The splashing, gurgling noise of the river seemed to be competing with his loud cries for the boy.

As the evening passed by Raicharans' mistress became very anxious. She sent men out to search for Raicharan and her little boy. The servants went with lanterns in their hands and as they reached the banks of the river, they saw Raicharan rushing up and down like a wild storm, shouting in despair, "Little Master, little Master." Forcefully they took Raicharan home, and when he saw his mistress, he fell at her feet. She shook him and questioned him and repeatedly asked him where her baby was? He could hardly breathe, 'He didn't know, he had turned around, he didn't know,' he kept repeating again and again. The mother went wild with her grief and piteously implored him, "Raicharan, give me back my child, oh, please give me back my baby." And Raicharan beat his forehead on the ground in total anguish.

A couple of days later Anukul ordered him out of the house, so Raicharan returned to his wife, without his heart or soul. One day just moved into the next, time no longer mattered, and then one day his wife told him she was with child. Raicharan did think, "How could this be, we are both so much older now?" But he said nothing to his wife. Before the end of that first year his wife gave birth to a son and died.

Raicharan looked at the infant and his mind became flooded with memories of another baby.

His sister called the baby Phailna and took care of him. But then, after a few weeks, a change gradually came over Raicharan's mind, and a wonderful thing happened. He saw in this baby another baby and when he heard his gurgling, his heart began to thump wildly against his ribs, and he felt like his former self again as he lifted the child up and held him close to his chest.

The baby grew quickly, and the years passed and soon it was time for Phailna to start school, and then Raicharan felt compelled to do what he knew in his heart he had to do.

He told his family that he was taking the boy to Calcutta to get him a better education, and they left their village.

But Raicharan did not go to Calcutta, instead he went to Baraset where Anukul lived and asked to see the mistress, who had had no other child, and was still broken down with grief.

When Anukul and his wife approached Raicharan he put his hands together and bent low and said, "It was I that stole your baby."

Anukuls' wife gasped and said, "Oh God, where is he?",

"He is with me," said Raicharan, and he stepped out into the courtyard and returned leading Phailna by the hand. Anukuls' wife took the boy into her arms, kissing his hair and his forehead all the while gazing into his face with hungry, eager eyes. Anukul looked at them and his heart brimmed over with a rush of sudden affection, but he said, "How do we know this is our child, have you any proof?" And Raicharan said, "How can there be any proof of such a deed. I alone know that I stole your boy."

Phailna had felt instinctively drawn to these two people, now, on hearing this, he understood why at times Raicharan had seemed so cold and distanced from him. He had never felt the love of a mother before, and now there was an instant bonding between the two like the deep love between a mother and her child.

Without saying another word Raicharan prostrated himself before his old master and mistress, then stood up and departed, never to be seen by any of them again.

In this story the servant knew in his heart what he had to do to make up for the devastating grief he had caused two people, whom he loved dearly, in a moment of negligence. Even though what he told them was not the literal truth it was the truth of his inner voice to make amends.

It was a sacrifice he felt compelled to make.

Jesus said, "The Truth will set you free," which can be interpreted as the unleashing of the Vishuddha chakra. When we speak the truth the energy within us can flow freely. We have nothing more to fear. Lies, along with fear, keep this chakra blocked.

Many years ago, when we were living in Singapore, my family and I had to live through a dreadful experience. One day we left our two-year-old son asleep with the Amah, baby-sitter, whilst my husband and I went shopping. Our older son was attending kindergarten. On our return home, as soon as we drove into our driveway, I knew something was wrong.

We opened the front door to find the place a mess, I screamed out to my son and the Amah, as I raced around frantically from room to room, I found our Amah gagged and tied to the legs of the bed, but she did not know where our son was.

She told me that three young men had broken into the house and that after tying her to the bed they had taken our little boy out of the room, whilst he was crying loudly.

We found our son in a spare room in a cupboard. He was curled up in the foetal position and he just stared at me, not a single sound did he utter. Fear had robbed him of all his speech and emotions. We raced him to a doctor, who told us there was nothing he could do for him. Physically he was not hurt, apart from severe bruising around his throat where the robbers had tied a plastic strap around his neck to stop him from screaming before they locked him in the cupboard. From a chatty, bubbly little boy we now had a silent child.

I returned to Australia to have an E.N.T. Specialist look at him, but he said the bruising on his throat was not the cause of his inability to speak, and even though his vocal cords were bruised, the main reason for his silence was because he had been traumatized. If, and when, he spoke again depended entirely upon his state of mind, as it was fear that had paralysed his vocal-chords. From that moment on I never let my son out of my sight. We did everything together, I played a lot of music, and I sang and danced with him to distract his mind from fearful thoughts.

I meditated often with him, just holding him close and praying and I made sure he spent a lot of time outdoors, under the blue sky, wearing blue shirts, and swimming in blue water.

Gradually he started to respond to us, his older brother made him laugh, first it was through simple sounds and gestures and then slowly his speech returned; and today my son is a confident public speaker.

I believe that it was the internal energy from this chakra that made him well again.

More recently, when I was taking a walk one evening, I saw an elderly man and a woman in their front garden. I smiled at them and said, "Hello," the woman immediately looked away, but the man returned my greeting. After that, every time I went walking the man always waved and said, "Hello," but never the woman. She always acted like she had not seen me.

Then for a while I did not see either of them.

One day I noticed a young woman in their garden, so I asked her whether she knew what had happened to the old couple who lived there. She said that they were her parents and that her father had died a month ago and her mother was in a nursing home. I told her I was sorry to hear her sad news, and that her father had been such a friendly man.

Her answer totally astounded me when she said, "Please don't feel sorry for me; we are all so relieved that he's dead, he was a nasty, cruel man."

No wonder that old woman could not even bring herself to call out, "Hello."

She was living a life of fear and had become so confined in it that she looked at everyone else with the same feeling—one of fear.

This verse from the teachings of the Buddha (Bodhidharma) sums it up nicely. "If you are afraid, you are in error. If you know how to calm your spirit and keep it still in all circumstances, you are in truth. Pray you will know how to calm your spirit and keep it still, in all circumstances." Doing this energises the Vishuddha chakra and our lives will be free from fear.

The expression 'that's hard to swallow' is often used when someone doubts the truthfulness of the spoken word. When the Vishuddha chakra is open you will not be taken in by others lies, in other words, you will not be so gullible.

Someone I worked with once told me how her partner often came home with extra money from job's he said he did at work. Somehow, she always felt uncomfortable about this extra money.

She found his explanation of how he got it 'hard to swallow.'

Then one day the police arrived at his work-place and arrested him for stealing. Her intuition had pre-warned her. She supported him throughout his ordeal because he was truly remorseful.

This verbal act of saying sorry is called repentance in many religious faiths. It is a powerful word because every time we say sorry for hurting someone, it will open this chakra. People often cry when they say sorry because the emotions are stronger when this energy is released from the Vishuddha chakra.

We know that our thoughts, actions, and words are dominated by our five senses and four out of these five senses smell, taste, hearing, and touch, are physically linked to the Vishuddha chakra. This link, or interconnectedness, of this energy centre is via all the thousands of sensory nerves that take information from the sense organs to the brain.

When we unblock the energy from this centre, we automatically get control over all the nerves in the vicinity of the Vishuddha chakra; this gives us control over the mind via the messages that the nerves carry from our senses to the brain.

Here is a simple explanation of how these senses operate.

Inside the nasal cavity there are many nerves, so when the molecules carrying the scent travel through the nasal cavity, they touch the nerves, and the nerves send messages to the brain which lets us know what we smell. It is the same with hearing. The inner ear is filled with fluid and nerves, so when the waves of fluid move across the nerves, they carry messages to the brain which interprets what we are hearing. This is what occurs in our normal unconscious state when the autonomic nervous system has the nerves busily sending messages regardless of whether they give us pleasure or pain. This indiscriminate action becomes an over-abundance of nervous energy especially during traumatic situations which causes stress (chaos) in the brain. Now when the messages that are carried by the nerves to the brain are consciously selected, we are then in control of this bodily function. It is no longer an automatic, indiscriminate action by the nerves and the mind, but a self-controlled action. This is when the body and mind are working together for the good of the self.

The energy from this chakra feeds, nourishes and controls the nerves in a heightened manner when we consciously work at unblocking it; this will give us freedom from our sense dominated mind to a more controlled Self.

The exercise I mentioned earlier of placing a cut orange up to your nose and not smelling it, but you are still breathing is giving you control over the senses. Doing this gives us self -control and makes us stand in our own power.

In yoga it is called Pratyahara, withdrawal of the senses.

When we control our senses, we can control our speech too.

'Sticks and stones can break my bones, but words can never harm me' is truly absurd. Words can do as much damage to a person's wellbeing as physical abuse.

At times it is necessary to be honest and frank with our speech, even when we know that it is not what the person wants to hear. There is an old Hebrew phrase—

"The sayings of wise men are like the sharp sticks that shepherds use to guide sheep."

Sometimes it is necessary to prod people, with our words, in the right direction but it must always be said wisely and compassionately. Loud verbal abuse stems from the lower level of our human energy, whereas calm, intelligent words arise from our higher Self.

Often, when drunken people are involved in a conversation, it is usually loud and often senseless. That is because excessive alcohol blocks this energy-centre and the senseless human nature is left to function alone.

A powerful speaker uses the energy from the Vishuddha chakra. By powerful I mean inspirational—some speakers inspire and motivate others into being more productive and more compassionate. They leave their listeners feeling elated and stimulated.

The bestselling author Louise Hay, in her book You Can Heal Your Life refers to the throat as 'the avenue of expression and the channel of creativity.' She says that when we express ourselves joyfully, and are willing to change, we will eradicate throat problems.

In other words, arguments, senseless discussions, and constantly reprimanding children can decrease the energy flow in this area. So, the person becomes more susceptible to illness, because the energy to attack the harmful bugs is diminished. In fact, constant bickering and arguments can completely block this chakra due to the excessive amount of negativity flowing through the throat.

Parents and teachers sometimes experience a lot of negativity in their environment. This makes it hard to experience any peace and joy; this is when change needs to occur even if it involves something as radical as moving away when all other avenues of help and constructive strategies have failed. It is paramount that the Vishuddha chakra stays open so that the energy from the Anahata chakra, pure love can flow through—our capacity to love must always be increasing, never decreasing, because love allows our words to be meaningful and truthful.

There is an ancient Israelite story about the prophet Elisha who taught and healed, in the spirit, meaning psychic gift.

One day an army officer named Naaman came to see him because he had a dreadful skin disease. Elisha was extremely busy, so he told his servant Gehazi to tell Naaman he would be cured if he washed himself in the river Jordan seven times.

Naaman was annoyed that Elisha had not come out to see him personally, and he had no faith in this remedy of bobbing up and down in the river seven times. He sent Gehazi back to tell Elisha that he was an especially important man and that he had gold and silver and fine clothes to reward him with, if he cured his skin disease. He said that even if Elisha could not see him personally, perhaps he could give him some herbal ointment to apply to the infected skin.

Gehazi returned to Naaman and told him Elisha was still too busy to see him nor did he have any ointment to cure him with and that the only remedy was to wash himself seven times in the river Jordan. On hearing this Naaman was furious and decided to keep his gifts and return home.

But one of his soldiers said, 'Master, what have you got to lose, it's a warm day and washing in the river will refresh you."

So reluctantly Naaman undressed and walked into the river Jordan.

After bobbing up and down seven times he stepped out of the river and found that his skin was completely healed.

He was so overjoyed that he raced back to Elisha with his gifts of gold and silver and fine clothes, but Elisha refused them saying he had no use for them. So Naaman left with his soldiers and gifts.

He had not gone far when his soldiers noticed Gehazi racing after them. Breathless, he told Naaman that Elisha had just received some unexpected guests so had changed his mind and would like the gifts after all. Naaman happily gave the gifts, even insisting that his soldiers carry them back for him. Gehazi had them placed in his house, and then returned to Elisha who asked him where he had been and Gehazi replied, "Oh, I had a few chores to complete."

Then Elisha said to him, "Don't you know that I was there in spirit when you accepted the money and clothes, and didn't I tell you that this was not the time to accept gifts?"

Gehazi left in shame. A few days later he noticed he had the same skin disease that Naaman had. The Biblical writers used this story to point out the harmfulness of telling lies, even though Gehazi most probably got the disease from wearing Naaman's infected clothes.

Lies block divine energy and that is why throughout the ages people have tried to emphasise the importance of truthfulness through stories whether they were fact or fiction.

One such tale is Pinocchio. Every time Pinocchio lied to the blue fairy his nose grew longer.

The connection here to the throat, speaking lies, the nose, getting longer, and the blue fairy is quite amazing when we think of the Vishuddha chakra.

Could the author have been aware of the blocking of this chakra when we resort to lies when he wrote the story of Pinocchio?

Remember one lie usually leads to another because the fear of being exposed dominates, so more lies are told to cover up the first ones.

The phrase, "Oh, what a tangled web we weave when first we practise to deceive", is so true.

A pack of lies can cause havoc in our lives!

Ironically, when Pinocchio finally speaks the truth, the blue fairy sets him free.

From this centre we communicate our wisdom, emotions, and creativity to the external world. When this chakra is open people see us as people of honesty and integrity. There is nothing to hide; we have no secrets. Relationships between couples work well when this chakra is open because this energy creates honesty and trust between them.

The Vishuddha chakra is the physic centre for people who hear voices and receive messages from the spirit world, referred to as clairaudience. The voices and messages will become even clearer when special attention is given to this chakra.

Whilst meditating on this chakra use eucalyptus or sage oil in a burner to further enhance the breathing and clearing of the nasal and throat passages. Remember the ears, nose and throat are all connected with this energy centre, which also helps to eliminate pain and stiffness in the neck and shoulders, because when it is flowing freely it massages and relaxes the muscles and nerves in this area.

Hindus use the image of the elephant as a symbol to remain focused on this chakra, which is understandable when one considers the remarkable elephant's trunk, which is its nose for breathing, its arm for feeding, and a straw for sucking up water to squirt into its mouth.

Its trunk is strong enough to pull down a tree yet sensitive enough to pick up a small coin.

So, the energy from the Vishuddha chakra is seen as powerful as the elephants' trunk, words of authority, and as gentle as the elephant's trunk, words of comfort.

One of the Biblical writers says, "I tried to find comforting words, but the words I write are honest."

Always remember the saying, "Honesty is the best policy," to keep this chakra unblocked.

Here is a true story of an unusual type of honesty.

A nephew of mine was on a business trip in Milan, Italy. One morning as he was hurriedly walking to an appointment, he was accosted by a family of gypsies who asked him for some money. My nephew said: "Sorry no," and walked on briskly, he did not want them to see the large amount of money he was carrying in his wallet, afraid that they would steal the lot if he attempted to hand over a few Euro dollars.

He had not gone far when he felt a tap on his shoulder. When he turned around, he saw that it was one of the gypsies whom he had seen previously with his wallet in his hand.

My nephew silently took it from him, amazed as to how they had taken it from him without him having the slightest inkling that they had retrieved it from the inner pocket of his jacket over which he was wearing a large, heavy coat!

When he checked his wallet a few minutes later, in the safety of his office, he found all his credit cards and the large amount of money still there except for one fifty-dollar note.

Hindu's practise singing the Om sound, called Amen in Christianity and Islam, to further activate this iridescent blue whirlpool of energy. The sound it creates within causes the bones in the inner ear to vibrate with energy from this chakra. These bones pass on the sound into a tube filled with fluid and this causes electrical messages to travel along the auditory nerve to the brain. This is believed to be the best way to strengthen the bones in the inner ear because the sound causes a unique type of vibration on the membrane of the eardrum. Singing the Om is a spiritual expression that has significant physical benefits. It improves auditory functioning and strengthens the vocal cords. So, sing the Om or Amen to further activate this chakra.

From the Vishuddha chakra we move up to the Ajna chakra.

This energy centre is found in the middle of the forehead, just above the eyebrows.

Mystics refer to it as the third eye and it is part of our pineal gland, a mystery organ to our medical profession even today but it is still visible and useable in some simple fish, like the lamprey, where the pineal gland is unmistakably a third eye with a lens and a retina.

People throughout the ages have tried to draw attention to this energy centre by placing a coloured stone or painting a mark in the middle of a deity's forehead. There are many statues of Buddha with this centre clearly defined. Sometimes it is a woolly curl, at other times it is represented by a single jewel, interpreted by Buddhists as the eye of wisdom.

The Ajna chakra, like the Vishuddha chakra, is connected to our higher Self, more to our spiritual nature than our human nature. Faith in our Self and in the Divine becomes unshakeable. The Ajna chakra is represented by the rich, deep blue colour called indigo, which is a strong colour dye. The dye is made from the powder of the indigo plant and can only be melted at 392 degrees centigrade.

In India, the plant is used to heal ulcers and abscesses, liver, kidney, and lung disorders and even some forms of cancer. In religious ceremonies the oil is extracted from the seeds and used to anoint the brow to open this chakra for spiritual growth.

In Australia, the headman of the indigenous people of the Kurdaitcha tribe placed a mark on the tribesman's forehead to build up their spiritual powers. They believed this gave them greater insight and wisdom.

In Christianity, the baptism ceremony is signified by the priest making the sign of the cross using oil on the forehead.

Judith Collins, Australia's leading authority on the human aura, tells us that when the Ajna chakra is activated she can see rays of indigo penetrating several layers of a person's aura.

The colour indigo is the sixth colour in the rainbow, and this is the sixth chakra of the major chakras where mystics say our sixth sense, called insight, is located.

It is also connected to our fifth sense, sight, and the energy from the Ajna chakra improves our physical eyesight by energizing the tiny nerves behind the eyeballs, with the added gift of insight, commonly called clairvoyance. Sometimes we experience this via our dreams.

My mother, in her eighties, had a dream that her granddaughter was pregnant. The next day, unaware at that time it had been a dream and feeling pleased about the pregnancy, she phoned her granddaughter to find out when the baby was due—in her mind she was nearly six months pregnant. Her granddaughter just laughed and said, "No Gran, I'm not pregnant at all, where did you hear that from?" So, my mother phoned two of her daughters—neither of them had told her anything, so she said, "Oh, I must have dreamt it."

A fortnight later my sister phoned my mother to say that her youngest son was in shock; his girlfriend had just told him that she was six months pregnant with his child.

The insight from this chakra gives us the wisdom to take responsibility for all of our life's experiences. As adults we do not have to blindly follow someone else's instructions or ideas or ways of how we should live our lives because each one of us has been given the gift of free will. The acts of terrorism that are committed by people who blindly follow a cause even when their actions bring about immense suffering to others are caused by a blocked Ajna chakra.

The energy from this chakra gives us hindsight so that we can see the results of our actions before they are committed. By seeing the bigger picture, we can draw positive experiences into our own life and into the lives of others.

Some people believe that people who instigate acts of terrorism are retaliating against other countries wealth and affluence. When we crave 'things' others have got we are seeing with our external eyes only. When we look from within, we are untroubled by materialistic possessions, we count our blessings in what we can give rather than in what we can receive and the wealth of another person, family or nation is not what we crave or covet.

A senior partner in a law practice, Warren Scott, wrote this in the Quadrant newsletter,

"We need to articulate that goal of an egalitarian society is not, and should not be, to reduce everyone to one common equal plane. But rather we should allow every member of society an equal opportunity to use their talents. Let us not fall into the trap of thinking that our goal is to make everyone equal, rather than treat everyone equally."

The energy from this chakra gives us a clear vision of how to lead, or how to follow.

Acts of brutality, dominance and terrorism are not from this source of spiritual energy. Any act, large or small, that is harmful to mankind is a denial of this inner vision.

And whilst we are busy condemning the perpetrators of inhumane acts of destruction, we need to look within ourselves at our own weaknesses and check out whether our words and actions have an ulterior motive.

The great master Jesus told his followers:

"Remove the log first from your own eye, before you see the speck in your brother's eye."

And in the ancient stories of Greek and Roman mythology, the giant Cyclops could see things with the eye in the middle of their forehead that no one else could see, so they made a helmet for Pluto that made him invisible to everyone except themselves.

The word Cyclops means, wheel-eyed, and the Sanskrit word Ajna means command wheel.

When the Ajna chakra is fully opened it synchronizes with the Vishuddha chakra and the Anahata chakra and gives us the wisdom to make wise choices.

These words from the Sacred Book of Taoism:

'He who is learned is not wise; he who is wise is not learned,' shows us that to blindly learn and believe something that another has written or said is unwise.

Knowledge from a limited perspective creates our fears and keeps us in the dark.

When we open our eyes and see the big picture our fears dissipate, in the same way that light destroys darkness. When we look at something we are seeing light that bounces off an object into our eyes. This light reaches tiny nerves, there are about 130 million nerve cells located here, which then carry the messages to the brain; it all happens so quickly yet we are totally unconscious of this occurring behind our eyeballs. This frantic activity of the nerves causes electric currents to flow from the retina to the brain along the optic nerves at amazing speed. Imagine having a third eye, outwardly invisible, that has so much energy in the nerve cells when activated it can create super visionary power. According to Yogis this is about seventy thousand times more powerful than the energy behind our normal eyes! When we focus our breathing into the third eye during meditation the energy in this centre will be activated.

Always bear in mind though that the energy from these centres cannot be used when they are blocked. Only when this energy is available to us can we use it to heal the body and mind.

Then not only does our physical eyesight improve, but we are also blessed with the gift of super sensory vision. This unique gift that has been bestowed upon people, often referred to as psychics and mediums, since the beginning of time was given to remove the blind-spots as we travel along the path of life.

Nostradamus, who lived in France 500 years ago, said he saw things not from his ordinary eyes. After his wife and two children died of the plague, he became so heartbroken he would sit for hours in quiet contemplation. One day whilst gazing absentmindedly into a bowl of water he began to see things. He decided to record these visions whilst in this trance-like state, and some of his most famous recordings were:

The Great fire of London in 1666.
The beheading of King Louis XVI and Marie Antoinette in
The French Revolution (1793)

The birth, rise and defeat of Napoleon.
The coming of Hitler in Germany.
The Second World-War.
The invention of radio and television.
The assassination of John F. Kennedy.
The destruction of New York City.

In 1554 Nostradamus told his friends he had only another twelve years to live and asked that a particular metal plate be placed in his coffin with his body. He died in 1566 and his companions fulfilled his request by placing the wrapped metal plate inside his coffin.

In the year 1700, a hundred and thirty-four years later, the authorities decided to move his coffin to a new tomb. Whilst in the process of moving the coffin they dislodged the metal plate to find only the number 1700 inscribed on it.

Nostradamus was inspired through his inner vision to write his bestselling book Centuries in the same way that countless other writers, artists, composers, and inventors have done throughout the centuries.

Virgil Brock, who wrote that beautiful hymn, Beyond the Sunset, got his inspiration from the inner vision of a blind guest. Whilst the two of them were sitting together chatting near a lake on a warm summer's evening Virgil was amazed when his blind companion said, "I've never seen a more beautiful sunset." Whilst he pondered upon the idea of his blind guest seeing, what was a glorious sunset, his companion said, "I can see, and I think I often see more. I see beyond the sunset." Virgil's blind guest was using his sixth sense of inner perception to see and feel that special sunset. And Claude Monet, in his eighties and almost blind, painted his largest work of art, Nymphaea with this super-sensory vision.

In the Bible, after Moses had given the Israelites the commandments, he told them to keep the commandments, 'as frontlets between your eyes'.

Moses was acknowledging the inner power of this chakra, so that his people saw the commandments not only with their physical eyes but also with deeper vision.

Jesus said, "The eye is the lamp of the body, so if your eye is sound, your whole body will be full of light. But if your eye is not sound, your whole body will be full of darkness."

Here the reference is to a singular eye, that of the inner vision of the third eye.

People who can see auras, colours of light that radiate from our body externally, see them through this super sensory vision. This luminous, subtle light of the aura's electromagnetic field, that encompasses our whole being, is more intense when the energy from the Ajna chakra is flowing freely.

William Blake, the great writer from the 18th century said,

"He whose face gives no light, shall never become a star."

How then can we unblock this centre to gain access to this infinite source of energy and light? Firstly, in all our dealings we must retain our honesty.

Hindu sadhus believe that people who are guilty of deceit and dishonesty during their working life will suffer from physical blindness in later life through a blocked Ajna chakra. No form of dishonesty goes by unrecorded in our mind, with the mind eventually making it more acceptable and justifiable so the dishonest pattern continues. Hindu sadhus teach their disciples to

"Be like the Lotus flower pure and untouched by the slush around you,' and 'when there is darkness all around, the single lamp, which sheds light, will be extraordinarily strong and enduring."

Honesty is a virtue that surpasses all others. Hindus call it the light of Mahamaya.

Often, we cannot see the wrong or the harm that our dishonesty does to others. We play the game of profit and greed and power, totally oblivious to the long-term ill effects this behaviour is having on the whole planet.

Buddhism teaches, 'what cannot be perceived can be reached only by curbing natural desires,'

in other words, our perception is extended when we control our selfish nature, the most common reason for people's dishonesty. Once dishonesty pollutes the mind, we will never achieve our life's aim, which is to evolve spiritually.

No matter what predicament or circumstances we are in we must always maintain our honesty. If it is a divorce settlement, be fair. If selling goods, do not rip anyone off because they do not know any better. In business make sure that money received has been rightly earned, do not take extra money if you think you can get away with it because in the long term you never do. The great train -robber Ronald Biggs stole a lot of money in Britain. He was caught and given a prison sentence, but he escaped and fled to Australia. When the Australian authorities were onto him, he fled to Brazil. As he got older, and his health started to fail he realized stealing that money was the biggest mistake of his life. He decided that he had to serve his time for doing the crime, so he returned to Britain and is now serving out his sentence.

His son, Mike Briggs said in an interview that the one thing his father had taught him was the value of honesty. This shows that Ronald Biggs does not want his son to repeat his mistakes.

To admit one's errors and to say sorry and seek forgiveness clears this chakra and allows this energy to shine through. This act of repentance also clears the Karma for the person's next life. Anyone who commits an act of dishonesty yet adamantly insists that they are guiltless, are creating a greater form of bondage for themselves.

Hindu's call this Maya and say that they are like the fish that are caught in the fisherman's net, yet bury themselves in the mud, thinking they are safe; because the initial freedom they feel is usually short-lived followed by long periods of despair,

The energy from this chakra endows us with a clear vision of how to live our lives because when we are honest, we are also trustworthy and truthful; we follow the lead of moral behaviour that gives us self-respect and this, flows into respect for others.

This Self-realization will not allow us to participate in any form of dishonesty; nor will it allow us to turn a blind eye to acts of dishonesty committed by others.

Use the wisdom from within when dealing with dishonest people and even if it earns us more censure than praise, in the long run promoting our principles will be beneficial to everyone.

It is called self-loyalty. I remember once in a supermarket the check-out girl gave a bag of groceries to a lady who immediately handed the bag back saying, "These are not mine."

Remember, whether it is a big deal or a little deal, stay honest, because when this chakra is fully open, we will receive all the benefits and blessings this universe has to offer and will not need for anything. We do not have to be dishonest to survive or live well; the power from this chakra leads us to many successful and fulfilling ways of making money to supply all our needs. As parents we need to set a good example to our children about the priceless value of honesty. I've seen young children 'tricking' others by stealing that which is not theirs, through cheating and lying, with some adults actually encouraging this type of behaviour by calling it cute and clever. Children need to learn that anything gained or earned fairly is the way to go on their journey of life. My son was exposed to an act of honesty at an early age.

I parked outside the bank one day and went in to do some quick banking leaving my eight-year-old son sitting in the car. When I returned, he was out of the car collecting money along the kerb, literally hundreds of dollar notes that were being blown about by a soft breeze.

He could hardly hold them in his hands.

With a look of total amazement he said, "Mum, look at all this money."

There was no one else around at the time and my car was the only one parked outside the bank.

I told him to go into the bank and hand it in to a bank teller because someone must have accidentally dropped the money because in those days most bills were paid for with cash.

When he got back to the car, he told me that when he was walking out of the bank, he saw a man rushing in looking very worried, we guessed it was his money.

Dishonesty usually stems from greed and a desire for more and more worldly possessions.

What the eyes see the mind wants and this wanting ensnares the mind to such an extent that it never stops wanting.

Buddhists say, wanting, is like drinking a cup of salt water—it just makes us thirstier."

There is an old folktale called, The Fisherman and the Goldfish, which I recommend parents read to their children so that they can get a better understanding of the wrong of wanting.

I feel that these fairy tales have a good reason for being in the world and for lasting through the passage of time.

There once lived an old man and his wife on the shores of the deep blue ocean in a little shack. The old man used to fish for his living and one morning he cast his net into the ocean and all he landed was one fish. But this was no common fish, it was golden, and it spoke,

"Put me back into the ocean, old man and I will give you whatever you ask."

The old man was astonished and frightened; he untangled the golden fish and put it back into the ocean. Then he hurried home to tell his wife about the incredible thing that had happened.

His wife got angry and said, "You silly, silly man, couldn't you at least have asked for a new wash-tub for ours is falling to pieces."

She scolded the man so much that he returned to the seashore and called out to the fish.

The golden fish swam up and said, "What are you wanting old man?"

The old man said, "My wife wants a new wash-tub," and the fish said, "It's as you wish."

The old man hurried home, and there was the new washtub.

The next day his wife said, "You silly man, you should have asked for something more than just a wash-tub? I want a new cottage."

So, the old man went back to the seashore and called out to the fish.

The fish swam up and said, "What are you wanting old man?"

The old man said, "My old woman wants a new cottage."

The fish said quietly, "Do not worry go home you can have a new cottage."

The man went back to his old shack and there in front of him was a new cottage with a fence around it and nice oak gates. But his wife was not happy.

Now she wanted to be a fine lady living in a tall mansion.

So, the old man returned to the seashore and called out to the fish.

The golden fish swam up and said, "What is it that you are wanting old man?"

The old man said, "My old woman gives me no rest. She wants to be a fine lady living in a mansion."

"She can have her mansion," murmured the golden fish. A week passed and the old woman grew prouder than ever. Then one morning she said to her husband,

"I am tired of being a fine lady I want to be a Queen and live in a grand palace."

And so, the old man went down to the seashore and called for the fish.

The golden fish swam up and said, "What is it old man, what is it that you are wanting?"

"My wife wants to be a Queen and live in a grand palace."

"Very well," said the fish and swam away.

The old fisherman hastened home and what did he see—a grand palace and in there he saw the Queen, his wife sitting on a throne.

A week later she sent for him and said, "I command you to go back to the golden fish and tell it I want to be Queen of the whole Earth, including the Seas."

Sadly, the old man set out for the seashore. He called out softly to the golden fish.

The fish swam up and said, "What is it that you are wanting, old man?"

The old man answered, "Forgive me Golden Fish, but my old woman now wants to be Queen of all the Earth even the blue ocean waters."

Not a word spoke the golden fish. It just swished its tail and in silence disappeared into the depths of the ocean.

The old man waited in vain for an answer and at last he turned his steps back for the palace.

But when he got back there was no palace; just his old shack and on the doorstep sat his wife, with the same broken washtub beside her.

Even though this story is a fairy tale it is relating to a truth. Many peoples' desire to accumulate more and more possessions leads them into debt. Then, to pay their bills, they sell their possessions and often end up with less than they had before. It also depicts so clearly the habitual pattern of wanting and how spiritually destructive that can be.

The saying, the more they get, the more they want, applies to us all because it is part of our human nature.

To all compulsive shoppers, those who want for the sake of wanting, try this simple exercise that will help you to distinguish between a want and a need. The next time you see something you want, close your eyes for a second and lightly place the fingertips of your left hand onto your third eye. Then open your eyes and remove your hand.

You will be amazed to find that your wanting has ceased and that you have clarity of mind as to whether the item in question is a want or whether it is needed for the well-being of yourself or others.

This exercise stops us craving unnecessary materialistic things that clutter up our lives.

We learn to see with appreciation, not with wanting. For example, we can look at a beautiful painting or a fine piece of jewellery, or a car and appreciate the creativity and craftsmanship that has gone into the object to create it, but we do not have the desire to own it.

The energy from this chakra teaches us how to use discernment in what we need and what we want. The only time that a want and a need go together is in having children. The desire for wanting a child is spiritually uplifting because it creates unselfishness in parents and the child fulfils the paternal and maternal needs of the couple.

Hindu priests anoint the brow of a woman who is trying to conceive, with oil from the indigo plant to stimulate the reproductive hormones, that are found in this area of the brain.

Judith Collins, a renowned Australian healer adds weight to this practice by saying:

> "I have noticed that in childless couples one or both partners have stifled their imaginative self, due to restrictions of one sort or another which causes a block in the third eye. When successfully treated, a child may be conceived."

From this chakra we move onto the seventh chakra.

In western culture there is the expression, Seventh Heaven. A perfect description for this spiritual energy centre because it connects us to that place of Eternal Bliss.

It is our crowning glory; its location being towards the crown of the head in that vital spot where the new baby's skull is not yet joined, often referred to as the soft spot.

Some mystics believe that the soul enters and leaves the human body from here.

Its Sanskrit name is Sahasrara, and it has been called the fountainhead of all spiritual and psychic phenomena. It is the centre for the development of our personality from where we evolve to a higher spiritual plane, and disciples of Tantra and Mantra believe that this chakra is the inexhaustible source of all philosophy.

The energy from this chakra transforms the brain and manifests a superior type of consciousness that has the greatest influence for good on our whole human life. It is referred to as the marvellous lotus of a thousand petals that holds the secret origins of all esoteric doctrines.

How then do we, mere mortals, gain access to this higher, purer form of energy that ancient seers have described as, "a circle of glowing radiance round the head;" and, "a gorgeous lotus of extraordinary brilliance, having a thousand petals to denote its large dimensions.'

When we unblock all the other chakras and reach enlightenment. This is when our energy and the Divine energy mingle as one.

This is the spiritual evolutionary process of the human mind when the negative inherited genes no longer dominate. The sins of the forefathers, seven generations back in Biblical writings, no longer apply. Their use by date expires when the energy from the Sahasrara chakra destroys those genetic traits that cause our addictions and weaknesses. We literally become free from genetic debilitating factors, and from environmental and cultural influences. This is the, born again experience, many have experienced. The genetically free personality, a personality that is so powerfully identifiable to that person no one can break it or change it. It is rock solid, in other words, it is built on a foundation of rock. Our identity becomes totally personalized, we are no longer 'just like Mum, or just like Dad, or Auntie Ivy, because the energy from this chakra has suppressed all those dominant genes and we are free from them; our thoughts and actions are governed by our newer, purer, stronger personality. Our only link to our inherited genes is in our physical appearance, not in the mind, that powerhouse for our thoughts and actions.

This revolutionary change manifests itself in every aspect of human activity and conduct. Our conscious mind now works in total harmony with our higher Self.

Tantric disciples need to undergo this complete change of personality through performing Sadhanas, holy practices for years on end, before they are recognized as competent teachers and/or priests of Tantra and mantra. They live their lives in simplicity and humility totally devoid of any egotism. Patanjali, a Brahman monk who translated the ancient Sanskrit philosophy of yoga, was according to W.B. Yeats, "a man who sought truth not by logic or moral precepts but by methods of meditation and contemplation that purify the soul; who replaced the trance of soma drinkers, or that induced by beaten drums or by ceremonial dancing, by a science that seems to me as reasonable as it must have seemed to its first discoverer, where the devotee attains a state of wakefulness called Samadhi, when the soul is purified of all that is not itself and it comes into possession of its own timelessness." (Dublin 1937)

"The enlightenment that comes to a Yogi at the last step is sevenfold." (Patanjali 3A.D.)

This is the complete person, the unity of the body, mind, and soul. It is reaching up to the seventh colour of the rainbow, purple.

The purple Amethyst enhances the energy of this chakra. This beautiful gemstone, created by nature over millions of years into crystals, has long been treasured by kings and queens as well as the hierarchy in religious sects. Its use can be traced back to the Minoan period in Greece to as far back as 2500BC.

Bryan Gardiner, who has done a significant amount of work on the healing properties of gemstones, says," the amethyst opens the path to the upper chakras removing illusions and bringing balance to the memory."

This balance of the memory is the spiritual unfolding of the conscious mind working with the super conscious mind, as a single unit.

When the Amethyst crystal is used during meditation it helps the energy to flow freely between the Ajna chakra and the Sahasrara chakra, to manifest spiritual unfolding.

Mystics believe that the Amethyst helps in easing the transition of the soul between life and death. Often an amethyst is placed near a dying person to activate their energy, so that the soul can travel peacefully on its heavenly journey. I read a story about an old cat that spent her last days lying near a large amethyst cluster.

This chakra is located near the brain in the area where the internal surfaces of the parietal and the temporal bones are formed between the middle meninges and its branches of nerve clusters.

The energy it supplies to the mind when it is activated is extremely powerful, thereby making it possible for the transformation of the mind and the personality to an altered and superior consciousness. Those who use the energy from the Sahasrara chakra have total control over the mind. They truly do have, mind over matter. It allows us to perceive things at a higher level of awareness.

Dr. Phil McGraw, a leading life strategist, says "we need to rethink how we think because it is our thoughts that govern our actions."

Tibetan Buddhists call it Tsul trim, the discipline of just action, or to do what is right. This, they say, will give us peace of mind.

But our personality needs to change before we can achieve this; because it is in our human nature to do what is best for us, rather than what is the right thing to do. When some of Jesus' followers were responding in a negative way, he told them,

"Your thoughts don't come from God, but from men."

This is the conflict between the conscious mind and the super conscious mind.

Dr Louise Hay says, "If we are willing to do the mental work almost anything can be healed." Keeping this chakra open through prayer and meditation will give us positive thoughts so we can release all thoughts of fear. Remember it is our thoughts that shape our life experiences. The energy from the Sahasrara chakra constantly steers us upwards to seek knowledge and dispel fear and this will change our whole attitude to life.

There will be no illusions, no expectations, because expectations reduce joy.

Expectation is a simple but extremely addictive thought process, because when we expect something to be wonderful, we nearly always end up disappointed and, conversely, when we expect the worst, we end up living in fear. Do not have any expectations, our minds are therefore left open, and we are free to respond with strength and ability in all situations.

Always remember that great expectations leave us unhappy and disappointed. Thoughts that are full of expectations are usually fictional, we fantasize about how wonderful things are going to be and then when reality strikes it confuses the mind. But because it prefers to recall those false thoughts of excitement, we are liable to repeat this pattern of mistakes again and again always living with the false hope that the outcome will be different the next time around. Einstein said: "Insanity is repeating the same action with the expectation of a different result." Psychologists and psychiatrists say that when we expect too much from others and ourselves, we live in a state of dissatisfaction which leads to depression.

Charles Dickens, some would say the greatest writer of the Victorian era, 1812-1870, wrote stories that were very realistic and sometimes sad. The sadness, I believe, came from his own expectations of how life should be.

His parents were well of so he was raised with the expectation that he would receive a good education at a Grammar School going on to Cambridge University, and one day live at Gad Hills Place, the finest house on the main road, between Rochester and Gravesend.

But his expectations were destroyed when his father, John Dickens fell into financial disaster and was imprisoned, and Charles had to go to work at Warren's Blackening Factory.

His expectations of marriage and love were also shattered when soon after his honeymoon his wife's sister, Mary Hogarth, came to live with them and he developed a deep fondness for her which lessened his feelings for his wife till it became almost non-existent.

One of the many stories written about him says: "Mary's death at seventeen years of age, in Dickens' arms, established in his mind an image of ideal womanhood, that never left him.'

He eventually separated from his wife.

It is no wonder that one of his greatest masterpieces was titled, Great Expectations.

In it, Dickens writes very realistically:
It was the best of time it was the worst of time.
It was the age of wisdom. It was the age of foolishness.
It was the season of light. It was the season of darkness.
It was the spring of hope. It was the winter of despair.

In his book The Old Curiosity Shop, Dickens' heroine is little Nell and her death, based on the death of Mary Hogarth, caused a nation to weep and sky rocketed sales of the book.

He became a success, even though his success was tinged with sadness due to his expectations. The crown chakra releases expectations and allows us to perceive each new situation or plan with clarity, without being too optimistic or pessimistic.

When Nathanael, a follower of Jesus, expressed to him his amazement that Jesus already knew so much about him before they had even met Jesus said,

"You shall see greater things than these; truly, truly, I say to you, you will see Heaven opened." When this energy is flowing freely it opens our mind to opportunities, and to new experiences, and to different modes of success coming into our lives.

We, have the ability, to understand our own thoughts and those of others coherently.

Confusion and the uneasy feelings of the mind are abolished. It is almost as if the individual self is constantly encompassed by a stupendous presence of wisdom and understanding.

Raymond Moody, who has done extensive work with people who have had near death experiences (NDE), constantly hears them say that while they were physically dead, they spoke with others but there were no words; it was a mental, instantaneous, communication.

The energy from the Sahasrara chakra enhances our powers of mental telepathy.

This chakra teaches us the lessons of humility and allows us to live a life of servitude without bondage. Mahatma Gandhi spent a lifetime serving others, from the illiterate labourers to the poor farmers, and was also a relentless crusader of women's equality and rights. He had this to say about service to others: "He who will serve the most will become the master of all. The only true gift is a piece of you."

Some of our great Kings and Queens have done just that, wearing their purple robes they have served their people. One of the greatest stories in Indian history is the story of the Rani of Jhansi, Lakshmi Bai who served her people gallantly until her death. She had seen and heard about the immense injustices that were committed to the Indian people who had submitted to British rule, and she felt it was her moral duty to save her people from the same fate after her husband's death.

For a woman of her time, she was extremely knowledgeable and had studied many of the ancient Sanskrit texts. But when negotiations between her and the invading British failed, she had no other option but to fight for her people and their freedom. Her conscious mind would not allow her to accept the terms of the invaders that would have allowed her to live in the lap of luxury while her people were reduced to slaves. For her, time would have turned their sorrow and misery into her own. She would never have felt proud or happy at acquiring her freedom at the expense of theirs. After much meditation and contemplation, she knew the path she had to take. The Rani had all her people from the nearby farms and villages brought into the fort that surrounded her palace. From this stronghold her people fought bravely against the British army, but their losses were heavy and after many weeks of fighting her soldiers were finding it harder and harder to protect her people. The Rani, who had been gallantly fighting alongside her men, realized that they could not hold out much longer. She felt their only hope was to try and get her people safely to Gwalior, some 200kms north, where the Raja had promised them safe sanctuary if she made it through the secret tunnel, out of the fort, into his kingdom.

Her people implored her to take her little son and escape, but this idea was as abhorrent to her as not protecting them was in the beginning.

She sent all of them through the tunnel, men, women, and children, whilst she, riding her horse with her son strapped to her, led the British soldiers away from the tunnel. She rode her horse at breathtaking speed along the high walls of the fort. She was riding on top of the wall! And then, just as the soldiers were closing in on her she took her horse over the wall—a hundred-metre drop. Incredibly her horse did not stumble or fall but galloped on through the forest with the Rani and the little boy safe on its back. Legend has it that she often rode guiding her horse with her knees whilst wielding her sword in her hands.

Sadly though, when she reached Gwalior, she had been betrayed and the British soldiers were waiting for her. Her death was swift, but her child's life was spared, and he was placed into the care of the Raja's household.

Apart from the sad loss of the Rani's life and others, another tragic waste that came out of this pathetic invasion was the looting and destruction of the Rani's palace by the British soldiers. They were so inflamed by the gall of that woman to stand up to their almighty power they burned all her ancient texts along with every book in her vast library in a huge bonfire.

Today all that remains of the Rani's vast wealth of books, art works and musical instruments is the sword she used in her final battle, and the clothes she was wearing at the time.

These can be seen at the museum in Gwalior. The first time I saw the sword I was struck by its immense size and weight, almost the same length as herself judging from the size of her clothes and apparently not much lighter than her body weight.

The power and stamina that this young, twenty-two-year-old Queen displayed compelled Sir Hugh Rose, the commander of the British forces at Jhansi, to record these words in his journal: 'The Rani was remarkable for her bravery, wisdom and perseverance. Her generosity to her people was unbounded.'

When we work with the energy from within our capabilities are unlimited. Here is another story of a brave Queen who used her great beauty to save her people.

Esther was a beautiful Jewish girl with large, dark expressive eyes framed by thick, dark, long eyelashes and her ivory skin was as smooth as silk. She had the kind of beauty that shone from the inside, out. Soon after she married the King, his chief adviser, Haman began to persecute the Jews. He manipulated the King through his lies and personal hatred towards all Jews to sign documents ordering their persecution.

Esther's uncle, Mordecai sent a secret message to her saying, "Go to the King and tell him that you are also Jewish and plead with him to save the lives of your people."

When Esther read the note, she began to tremble with fear and sadness. She thought, 'if I tell, the king I am Jewish he will send me away and take another Queen.'

For a while she lay on her bed thinking, 'No, I will never tell the King I am Jewish'.

Then, in the stillness of her room she felt a stirring in her heart and an immense sadness welled up within her for her people. She was shaken with grief and her heart went out to them in sympathy and then she heard a voice speak to her mind,

'Perhaps you have been made Queen for this very purpose.'

Esther lifted her head and felt her spirits rise. For three days she prayed and fasted and then she said, 'I will go to the King, even if I am to die for my people, then, let it be so.'

She rubbed sweet smelling oils on her skin, put on her red gown, and slowly made her way to the throne room. Her heart was pounding, but her dark eyes were steady and determined.

The King seemed to feel that she was there. The scent of her perfume filled the room. He turned his head slightly and saw her standing in the soft, shimmering light. She could never have imagined how lovely she looked. She was not aware of the grace with which she moved, as she knelt before the King.

Her beauty awakened feelings in his heart and a look of tenderness passed between them.

"What is it Esther?" the King said softly. Esther's heart began pounding again as she lowered her eyes and quietly answered, "I wish for the pleasure of your company at dinner this day."

"Yes, I would love to come," he answered.

The King visited Esther's chambers three times and each time he said, "Come now Esther, what is it you wish for me to give you?"

On the third visit the Queen also invited Haman. After dinner when the King again asked Esther whether there was anything she required she replied, "If you truly love me, then save my life and the lives of my people throughout your land, for there is a decree that all Jews are to be persecuted and killed." "Who would order such a cruel thing?" demanded the King.

"This man Haman," said Esther.

The King was furious and ordered that Haman be removed from his kingdom immediately. Esther felt a lightness descend upon her. All the worry and fear and the struggle for courage were behind her now. The King held out his hand to her and at that moment she knew that she was the fortunate recipient of divine grace.

King David of the Israelites wrote: 'You have made me ruler over the nations.

People I did not know have now become my subjects. Foreigners bow before me.

You give knowledge to me, your servant. '

David acknowledges his Kingship, but he also saw himself as a servant.

In our everyday lives we are all leaders who serve, irrespective of whether we have the purple robe and golden crown. Service is giving and we can all give in so many, many ways.

My sister's grandchildren call our mother GG, Great-grandmother, which aptly describes our mother; because she just keeps going and going; and she just keeps giving and giving.

When we humbly serve others, we too will be recipients of divine grace, that universal energy that will recharge our own energy and give us the strength to keep going and giving.

Volunteer groups are in all communities, joining a group will give you an opportunity to help others. A friend of mine recently offered some of her time to listen to people on the phone. I said to my friend "What do you say?" and she said, "Nothing much, I just listen, they are the ones who talk." She said people needed to express their feelings and for many talking over the phone, and to a stranger, was the only way they could. Talking on the phone helps them overcome some of their fears and anxieties.

Recently a woman was acknowledged for helping victims of abuse. People in the group asked what they could do to help, without the necessary qualifications, and all she asked them to do was to smile at others. She said that victims of abuse have extremely low self -esteem, so when someone smiles at them, they think that person must like me. Sometimes a smile is all it takes to make someone feel worthwhile. Yet smiling at anyone and everyone is not that easy to do, because in our society today we have cultivated the separation syndrome, caused by our material status that has given us a more aloof mentality. As a result, a lot less people in the affluent world are smiling today. Even children do not smile so readily and yet one of the most exciting moments in a parent's life is when their baby gives that first smile and then they spend countless hours trying to induce more smiles. When we try so hard in the beginning why don't we encourage and give it more readily in later life?

It is because changing our habitual patterns of thinking and behaving is not easy to do. But to grow, and for our personalities to evolve, we need to change our conditioned way of thinking, because change is growth and growth is life.

Look at the plants, they grow and change with the seasons when they stop changing, they die. The opening of the Sahasrara chakra helps us to understand and embrace change.

Buddha said: "There is only one law in the universe that never changes, that all things change."

This poem by Portia Nelson displays our foolish determination to resist change.

I walk down the street,
There is a deep hole in the street,
I fall in
It takes forever to get out.
I walk down the same street,
There is a deep hole in the street,
I fall in again,
It takes a long time to get out.
I walk down the same street,
There is the deep hole,
I still fall in-it is habit.
This time I get out immediately.
I walk down the same street,
There is a deep hole in the street,
I walk around it.
Later, much later, I walk down another street.
Stonebarn Publishers: *There's a Hole in my Sidewalk*
by Portia Nelson © 1989.

When we meditate, we reflect on our lives and are inspired to make changes without feeling fearful or uncomfortable. When we refuse to change, we shut off the possibility of learning from change and experiencing new growth, because with change comes greater self-realization and, as we let go of old habits and patterns that are no longer working for us, we will experience life in all its fullness.

Buddhists say that learning to live is learning to let go.

I read a story of a prisoner who after serving his time was released. He had not been in the community for long when he re-offended. When he was brought before the judge, he said that he wanted to be sent back to prison because that was where he felt safe.

They now have programs now to help prisoners who are released to adapt to living in the community again. The authorities found that the change for many prisoners from being on the inside to moving to the outside was too difficult to cope with, and that they were deliberately committing crimes so that they could get a prison sentence. Instead of welcoming freedom these prisoners fear it because it involves change.

The energy from the Sahasrara chakra gives us the power to emerge from change with a new strength and confidence.

Think of the metamorphosis of the butterfly. It begins life as this fat little caterpillar that just eats all day hardly moving. Then it goes into a deep sleep or retreat. It then transforms into this beautiful butterfly that flies away abounding with energy. The caterpillar's life totally changes. We must do the same, with wisdom and courage we must embrace all that life has to offer us. The energy from this chakra helps us to move like the wind and tide, standing strong in our own power knowing that our life is a deathless entity, and that we are woven inextricably with all of creation.

Our human nature is simply a collection of changing characteristics; this is the biological evolution of the mind, which is expedited through this crown chakra. A metamorphosis occurs within our nature, and, as our attitude changes, we enthusiastically embrace all new experiences, and live our lives for the good of ourselves and others.

This note, found written on a scrap of wrapping paper in the Ravensbruck concentration camp in Germany at the end of World War II, gives us an insight into the personality of an advanced soul; one that would radiate light from all the energy centres:

'Oh Lord remember not only the men and women of good will, but also those of ill will.

But do not only remember all the suffering they have inflicted upon us, remember the fruits we bore thanks to this suffering, and our comradeship, our loyalty, our humility, the courage, the generosity, the greatness of heart which has grown out of this.

And when they come to judgement, let the fruits that we have borne be their forgiveness.

We must all strive to acquire this greatness of heart and mind using the energy from the crown chakra that is part of the Divine energy, that measureless ocean of eternal wisdom.

Eileen Gable a psychic who receives channelled messages from the spiritual realm says that we should step aside from,' our calculating mind, and just let divine love and wisdom operate in you'.

Zen Buddhists use riddles like,' what is the sound of one hand clapping?' This contradicts people's usual pattern of logical thinking, and they think beyond preconceived ideas.

And Heraclitus, the Greek philosopher, stimulated the mind to understanding change when he said, "It is impossible to step into the same river twice."

This chakra is all about embracing change so we can spiritually evolve to a higher level of consciousness.

Jesus advised his disciples to seek a new path if the one they were on was hostile and detrimental to the wellbeing of themselves and others. And he took these instructions one step further when he told his disciples to even, 'shake off the dust from your sandals when you leave.'

These words imply a complete change with nothing from the past still clinging to us.

The energy from this chakra gives us the wisdom to make wise choices, which sometimes calls for a radical change in our life-style.

Laibi Wolf, an Orthodox Jewish Rabbi and the promoter of mind yoga has spent years researching the Jewish mystical tradition known as Kabbalah. He says the study of Kabbalah and its teachings of spiritual energy is a discipline which brings together the heart and mind in a fine balance. This is what automatically happens when the Anahata chakra works with the crown chakra. Laibi Wolf refers to the Sahasrara chakra as the spiritual fitness-centre and tells people, "Don't wait to gain wisdom just before you die. Do not even wait until mid-life crisis hits you. Do it now."

Rabbi Wolf believes humanity has reached a stage where the Kabbalah wisdom will be made available to all those who seek spiritual enlightenment. He believes that our mind is expanding to accommodate a higher level of intelligence.

But to tap into this source of intelligence we need to broaden our mind and accept the impossible as possible.

With people like Rabbi Wolf, and the many learned gurus and lamas to guide and teach us about these hidden mysteries, using the energy from this chakra to enhance our intuitive mind will become part of our daily lives. When we all tune in to our inner resources, we will eliminate the pain and suffering we now accept as, the way life is meant to be.

At some time in our lives, we have all experienced an intuitive moment that surpasses the conscious mind. I vividly remember my moment even though it occurred many years ago.

We were living in Taiwan in an apartment block that had a laneway between our block of units and the next. No cars travelled down that lane, so I allowed my son, who had recently turned five, to ride his bicycle directly in front of our apartment while I got the evening meal prepared.

One evening, whilst I was busily blending some vegetables in the food processor, I suddenly switched it off and literally ran over to the front room window just in time to see a man lifting my son's bicycle into the boot of his car. I screamed and ran out of that apartment and into the laneway just in time to see the car racing off, with the lid of the boot still up.

My son looked at me in surprise, with his bike lying thrown down in the middle of the lane. I was shaking like a leaf while he calmly told me that the man was going to take him for a ride in his car. My son told him he could not leave his bike in the lane, so the man got out of his car and was just about to put the bike into the boot of his car when I appeared at the window screaming. I knew at that instant had I not left my food preparation and raced to that window my son would have met with some horrendous fate.

I silently thanked God for what I believed to be an act of divine intervention that came to me via the crown chakra. These experiences in our lives are an indication of a higher consciousness at work. Somewhere in the depth of my mind I heard that man's car and knew what was about to take place and I responded, even though my conscious mind was occupied with my food preparation: As earthbound mortals we would not survive if we did not have this higher level of consciousness to guide us.

The Mayan people of South America used an amethyst skull to enhance the energy of this chakra. One found by archaeologists is the size of a normal human skull and carved from dark purple amethyst, with special indentations near the frontal lobe; maybe to represent the thinking side of our brain. This amazing skull absorbs light instead of reflecting it.

When meditating on this energy centre surround yourself with purple.

It has long been established by colour therapists that purple aids mind expansion and destroys unwanted patterns of behaviour. It also stimulates harmony and creates a feeling of being one with all.

Irene Sunn, a colour therapist at the Living Colour School in London says this about colour. "Each colour has its own strength and vibration.

And different colours can be used to balance the body's physical, emotional, mental, and spiritual energies, and restore it to natural vitality."

The ancient Egyptians and Greeks built colour healing temples.

The Chinese used colour for diagnostic purposes, the Tibetans combined colour with mandalas and meditations, and the Celtic people believed that the colour purple, along with the amethyst, transformed negativity.

These cultures recognized long ago that colour works on expanding the conscious mind.

Today, colours are getting greater recognition once again. Scientists at Flinders University in Adelaide, Australia have developed blue and green spectacles to eliminate jet lag.

These glasses help to decrease physical and mental fatigue, after travelling long distances, by re-setting the body clock in the mind.

Over the years I have noticed a strong fascination for the colour purple amongst young children and a lot of them will say that their favourite colour is purple. I believe that this is because they are still connected to the spiritual realm from where they have recently arrived.

Look out for a special sunset, when the colours lilac and purple fill the evening sky and quietly gaze upon it. Let your thoughts travel towards the transition between day and night.

That is how it is when we shift from one reality to the next, leaving us with no doubt about the validity of the super conscious mind.

Moving from our normal state of consciousness into super-consciousness is as easy as day turning into night when we use the energy from the chakras.

These chakras, along with the body's endocrine glands, link us with the elements—Earth, Water, Fire, Air and Ether, in a unique way. This connection between us and the elements affects us physically and emotionally through the feeding in of good energy and the disposing of unwanted energy.

Earth brings balance and healing to the Adrenal gland, also the Muladhara chakra, and brings joyfulness to the heart when functioning properly.

Today scientists agree to the link between this gland and the heart.

Water is linked to the ovaries and testes, which secrete fluid, and are responsible for creating life that begins in water. They are located near the Svadisthana chakra.

Fire, that generates heat through solar and volcanic energy, allows the pancreas to function effectively along with the Manipura chakra.

Air is connected to the Thymus gland and the Anahata chakra. This is the most important gland in an infant because it regulates the rhythm of the breath in newborn babies.

It is considered the breath of life.

Ether, that permeates all of space, is the element that allows the Thyroid gland to function.

It lies in the vicinity of the throat chakra and secretes a hormone that brings wellness to a person physically and emotionally.

Patanjali said, "Concentrate on the hollow of the throat; go beyond hunger and thirst."

All five elements work on the Pituitary and Pineal glands.

Their location, at the base of the brain, connects them to the Ajna and Sahasrara chakras through the nervous system, via the senses.

We know that our senses depend upon the elements to function; the nose depends on earth for smelling; the tongue depends upon water for tasting; the eyes depend upon light for seeing,

the ears depend upon air for hearing and the skin depends upon wind for touching. This interaction with the elements confirms the Hindu belief that whatever is in humankind is in the Universe, and that whatever is in the Universe is in humans.

The phrase, to be in one's element, indicates a totally adjusted happy human being, whereas being exposed to the elements, indicates a vulnerability to suffering from natural and super-natural forces.

Swami Umeshranand taught me these mantras to bring harmony to the body, mind, and soul. Learn them with a teacher, or add the r sound before the m, the mantra Lam sounds like Larm.

Chant them continuously for five minutes to bring inner peace and balance to the body and mind.

For the Earth mantra chant OM LAM.
Water OM VAM.

Fire OM RAM.
Air OM YAM.
Ether OM HAM.
For the Pituitary gland chant OM.

Pineal gland chant, OOOOO*h* (short h)—this chant also assists in opening the third eye. Sometimes, during the chanting of these mantras, a coloured light will be seen, whilst the eyes are closed, to match the chakra- for example you might see a green light whilst chanting Om Yam.

I hope this chapter has given you an understanding of the seven major chakras and their link to the endocrine glands with the elements.

Carefully study the drawing of where these energy centres are situated and place your hand on each energy centre in turn and think of it. Do this often, especially when taking a bath or shower and when you lie down and meditate, place a coloured piece of felt material on your body in these areas to further stimulate the energy of these chakras.

Chapter Four

OUR PERSONALITY'S PERSONAL TRIUMPH: LIVING IN PEACE: OM, SHANTI, SHANTI, SHANTI

I have been meditating for thirty years so it comes very easily to me. But I do realize that for some people it is quite a difficult process. You need to learn how to still the mind. Start with focus exercises.

Animals are good at this, have you ever watched an animal documentary of the tiger?

First the tiger will watch its prey, nothing moves, not even a whisker, it is totally focused, then it will pounce.

Focus helps to regulate and control our thoughts till we are free from all thoughts.

Jesus said, "In the stillness of the mind I will come to you."

When the mind is stilled we reach our higher Self.

Learning to focus the mind on just one thought at a time has untold benefits, especially in moments of crisis; because when the mind has an overload of thought patterns it causes us to react in an irrational manner, which then does us more harm than good.

I can remember having a nerve-racking experience many years ago when my thoughts were on the verge of becoming totally chaotic.

One night, as I got into my car to go and collect my husband from the airport, another car suddenly came into my driveway and stopped just behind my car and two men stepped out.

I immediately locked my car doors and sat in frozen silence while the two men banged on my car, yelling profanities, and demanding I open the door and get out.

Unable to drive the car anywhere, with a wall in front and their car behind, I was trapped.

I had an irresistible urge to sound the car horn, but my two sons were asleep inside the house and, being young teenagers, I was scared these men might attack them if they awoke and opened the door to investigate where I was.

The banging on my car and the filthy language continued with one obnoxious creep even urinating in front of my car.

Looking through my rear vision mirror I noticed a third man sitting in the driver's seat in the car behind me, so I switched my focus totally onto him.

All my thoughts and inner energy went into him, and while I gazed into the rear vision mirror, I repeated in my mind, go away, go away.

It became a silent chant with the words completely absorbing my mind.

In, what I believe, were a few seconds I heard him yell out, "Come on you two the F-- - - B- - is not going to get out. My focus became stronger, fear disappeared as all my energy went into those two words go away, and then they were gone!

A rush of conflicting thoughts entered my mind and for a second there was utter chaos in my mind, which was on the verge of giving into panic. 'Rush into the house,' I thought; 'No, one man might still be hiding somewhere, 'even though my eyes had seen them all leave.

'Don't move, just stay in the car, Ken will come home in a taxi from the airport and find me,'

'Drive off. No, they might be waiting in their car further up the road.

'Sound the car horn No it's still not safe for the boys.' My thoughts were jumbled and panicky.

Thoughts travel at amazing speed and during times of heightened emotions cause utter confusion in the mind that defies all logical thinking.

Then, my years of practicing focus exercises and meditation kicked in, and with total clarity I began to focus on three new words, 'go get Ken.'

After thinking these three words a few times I became aware of an extraordinary change in me.

I felt perfectly calm because my conscious mind was so relieved that it only had to deal with three simple words whilst the cognitive centre in my brain was saying, 'This is so easy to comprehend.'

Before this my mind had been on the verge of just freaking out. Now, "Go get Ken,' which I was chanting continuously, was precise, and easy to define due to its simplicity. So, I backed my car out, drove to the airport and picked up my husband. On the way home I told him about my experience with an outpouring of emotion because I felt safe in the security of his presence.

The following day I did a meditation with the focus being only on how well things had turned out and my thankfulness for that. That experience did not hamper my driving at night on my own in any way because my focus remained on the successful outcome of the situation, and that gave me confidence in my ability to handle stressful situations.

Edwin Land, an American inventor said,

"If you are able to state a problem it can be solved."

In other words, our abilities are unlimited when we go deep within to seek answers.

When the Yugoslav War Crimes Tribunal convened in The Hague, Antonio Cassese, the President, found it increasingly difficult to deal with the gruesome details of man's inhumanity towards the people in Bosnia.

To stay focused he would visit the Mauritshuis Museum and gaze at the beautiful paintings by Johannes Vermeer. Then he would return to The Hague feeling better equipped to handle the horrible stories that lay on his desk.

Children find it easier to focus than adults because their minds are not as clogged up as ours. Like children we need to unclog our minds. We need to let go of all those things that are distracting us from peacefulness.

One of the best ways to train yourself to focus is while you are performing simple tasks like peeling potatoes. Think only of the potato in your hand and the skin as it peels off, nothing else. Stop the mind from taking messages of what else the eyes see or the nose smells or the ears hear.

Shut down all the other senses, apart from using those sight nerves that are required for looking at the potato and even control the sight to seeing only the skin that is being peeled off, nothing else, even if it is connected to the potato. Each time your mind wanders away from the potato bring it back to the potato that you are peeling.

Practice makes perfect, so you will need to do a lot of focus exercises before you can successfully meditate.

Since children find it easy to focus, they find meditating easy too. At school I have found that a small colourful mat or cushion in a quiet spot is the ideal place for individual children to do a meditation. And it works well with children who have learning difficulties, behaviour problems or those who just want a quiet moment.

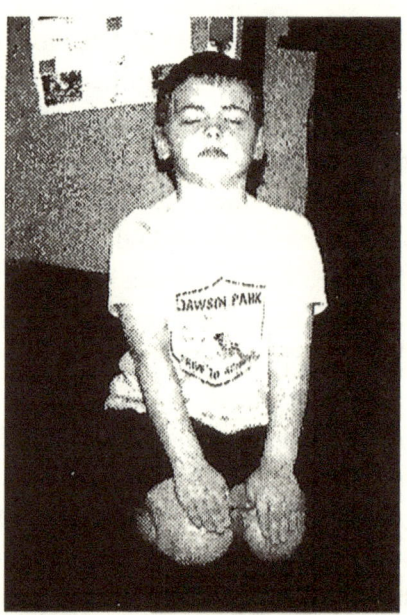

Encouraging the children to use simple yogic postures further helps in eliminating these unwanted problems. For behaviour problems, especially temper tantrums, ask the child to sit on their legs with them folded under their bottom so that they are sitting on the back of their calves with the knees bent. Sitting like this for a few minutes gives instant relief from physical and mental tiredness, which is very often the cause of temper tantrums in young children.

Near the mat have a small basket of semi-precious stones from which the child chooses one,

and this is a real plus—allow them to spray themselves with a water-spray containing a couple of drops of lavender before sitting on the mat. Tell them to focus on the stone in their hand with their eyes open or closed.

This concentrated focus shuts the mind down and the child experiences a peacefulness that helps them to cope with whatever they need to deal with at that time. Keep the time on the mat short, no more than five minutes, or the child will go to sleep.

So, parents instead of sending your child to their room send them to the Quiet Mat.

Make it an attractive spot, if possible, put a canopy of fine material over the top in their favourite colour, but do not allow it to become a play area, and let them sit in the Padmasana posture. Treat it as special and you will find that your child will take themselves to the mat whenever they feel the need to bring their body, mind, and soul into balance.

Learning to focus on just the task at hand makes it easier to do and it gets completed quicker too. Once you master this you will find that your thoughts will become clearer and more positive, because most of our negative thoughts come from an overworked mind.

As you build up this power to focus, you will develop a sense of peace and harmony in your life even under stressful conditions.

This is how it was for Shah Jahan when his son imprisoned him. He kept his focus on the unsurpassable beauty of the Taj Mahal—the beautiful white marble and the crystals, with its precious and semi-precious stones of lapis lazuli, jasper, carnelian, turquoise, agate, coral, diamonds, emeralds, rubies, sapphires. He looked at it, glistening in the midday sun and shimmering in the moonlight. He saw in it such amazing grace, moulded out of hard cold stone, yet warm and soft as his eternal love was for Mumtaz Mahal. While his focus was on such beauty and love he did not allow thoughts of hopelessness, revenge, or bitterness to fill his mind. Thoughts of his wife's death, the loss of his throne, his imprisonment, and added to all these was the gruesome experience of being sent the severed head of his first -born son, would have sent him insane.

But instead, he lived through the beauty of a building and his eternal love for his Queen.

Focus is concentrating but in a relaxed sort of way.

Gardening is excellent for this and has the extra bonus of connecting us to nature, especially when our hands and feet are bare, so the energy can flow freely from the soil and plants, and blend with our energy. Even weeding can be a calming experience when we stay focused.

When we master the art of focusing, we will begin to consciously use this skill in everything we do. This will allow us to draw on extra energy from within whenever we require it.

Try this exercise, when walking up a hill stay focused on your legs and feet, nothing else, and feel the strength in them. In no time at all you will reach the top, with seemingly little effort.

Then try walking up that same hill with your focus on the hill itself, and how steep it is.

When you reach the top, you will be a lot more breathless with aching legs and feet. Why? Because during the first walk uphill you summoned all the energy within your body into your feet and legs, thereby relaxing everything else so the breath remained normal with the mind believing it was an easy climb, because you did not tell it otherwise.

During the second walk up hill your inner energy was used up thinking about the steep climb ahead of you so your legs and feet did not receive that energy to help them carry the body up the hill.

It is amazing how much energy is used when we indulge in negative thinking, which leaves the body tired.

Focus exercises can also be used to lose weight. To start with begin by putting less and less food on the plate, then slowly eat each mouthful and stay focused on the food while it is in your mouth. Just before all the food is eaten start to feel very full in the stomach and just as the last spoonful goes into your mouth consciously think to yourself, "I cannot eat another morsel" and immediately take your focus elsewhere. This might require you to physically move into another room or even outdoors, I have found that brushing my teeth at this time excellent in shifting the conscious mind onto something else.

It is a documented fact that people eat more whilst watching television. This is because they are not focused on the food, so the mind does not know when to stop. When you switch your focus away from the television and stay focused on the food the eating addiction will stop because putting food into the mouth whilst watching television becomes a habitual pattern and because the mind loves patterns it will do it automatically.

You need to change the pattern to control the mind.

If you have the choice between eating an apple or a large slice of cake and you would much rather eat the latter but know it is not what your body needs focus on the apple. Smell it, see its crispness, and imagine the sweet taste. Then, eat it. You will enjoy it because the mind eventually gives in when we stay focused. To win the battle of the bulge draw on the energy from within and then what seemed like an impossible task becomes possible.

My mother in her eighties always asked for help to undo a bottle or jar or to lift items.

Things that she said were too hard for her to do.

Well, she was visiting with me one day and whilst strolling around on the back porch she saw something come towards her that scared her, so she raced inside and opened the door with such force it broke the catch and tore the door off one of its hinges.

My husband was so amazed, saying that he would have had difficulty removing the door off like that, yet this feeble woman when totally focused did it with ease.

And once I read a story of a woman lifting the back of her car to rescue her pet from underneath it.

When we learn to focus, not only will we have more strength but mentally we will be more alert, because we will be channelling all our energy into one specific area.

Jesus said that if we had enough faith, we could move mountains!

His speech often contained highly exaggerated terminology but what he was talking about was faith in our Self, because when we tap into our energy along with the Divine energy, we become powerful human beings.

Ralph Emerson (1803) said: "What lies behind us, and what lies before us, are tiny matters compared to what lies within us."

We lose a lot of energy when we relive the past or worry about the future because our thoughts are active, so they consume energy. We need to constantly focus on the present moment, forget about the past, and refrain from worrying about the future. Then the energy from within will enable us to go forward and feel confident that we can rise above any momentary problems, because in life when one door shuts another door opens. If we keep our focus on the door that has shut, we are unconsciously directing all our energies onto that closed door when what we should be doing is using all our energy to step forward, into the door that is wide open, and into new opportunities and experiences.

Our conscious mind will come up with all sorts of reasons why we should not look into that newer changing domain by reminding us about our, lack of money, or the disapproving words of another. It might even try to convince us that we are not physically or intellectually capable of stepping through that new door. Why?

Because the mind does not like change and here is an opportunity to do something new, so it will try to convince us otherwise with all sorts of reasons as to why we should not travel down that path. With the wisdom from within negative thought forms will be deleted.

We will go through the open door confident in our ability to embrace change, even though at first glimpse it appeared obscure, like the grey streaks of dawn; but then it will soon change into clear brightness just as it always does when the sun appears over the horizon.

Practitioners of Tantric yoga have established that we only use five percent of this internal energy in our daily lives.

To prove this, they perform certain yoga practices that require immense strength and focus which the average person cannot do, because they are unable to access this inner energy.

One of their most focused functions is in the sensual yogic techniques. It is seen as a form of erotic ritual, an emotional and physical expression of creation that links the human energy with the cosmic energy that pervades in every atom and molecule, in all the elements and compounds that are part of the earth's flaming core.

Through the long-continued practice of concentration they gain voluntary control over their nervous system, and this enables them to divert a greater flow of energy, prana, into the brain which results in an intensification of the sexual act. This fast moving, super physical activity measures the degree of proficiency in mind control and concentration. And as they extend the duration of the sexual act the sensual perceptions are heightened; this amplifies and refines the other senses and takes the conscious mind into the super-sensory realm which is the development of the super conscious regions of thought and perception.

In Tantric yoga, control of radiant energy between the chakras leads to transformation of the sexual urge into spiritual enlightenment. Tantric yogis maintain that the sexual act is a dominant aspect of our human nature and if suppressed brings a chemical imbalance to the brain. Thus, Tantric yoga promotes it as a necessary tool to achieve balance and control of the mind. This heightened level of focus, which many Hindus attain after reciting mantras and practicing correct breathing techniques, brings a couple into that moment of deeply shared intimacy when everything else in their environment melts in the warmth of closeness.

But this focus on the sexual act is for the advancement of the personality through the conscious control of the human mind; depravity or abuse of any kind is seen as a contamination of the mind thus a regression of the whole personality.

Practitioners of Tantra believe all acts of sexual depravity—rape, incest, paedophilia can be cured through yoga postures.

To cure this type of addictive behaviour patients must perform Siddhasana where they sit cross-legged on the floor with the left heel between the anus and the scrotum, and the right heel on top of the left heel, against the pubic bone. The body must be erect with the right palm of the hand on the left palm, near the right heel. The body is neither too tense nor too relaxed. This posture needs to be held for five minutes while prayers or mantras are chanted. This will bring balance and harmony to the body, mind, and soul. When they reach this higher level of consciousness all inappropriate sexual thoughts and actions will cease.

Whatever the task or activity its outcome must always be towards the improvement of our Self.

It should bring a sense of contentment and peace to the body and mind.

Swami Shri Purohit explains it like this,

"In the beginning the forces of the mind are scattered, the yogi tries to knit them together, tries to fix his attention on one object, to leave all others.

Then he succeeds in uniting his mind with that object, ultimately finds that both are finally dissolved in the Self.

In the same way element and sense lose their form.

There is the clay, the potter reduces it to fine powder, all particles separate from one another, he joins them by some binding material like water, gives it the shape of a vessel, uses it until broken, when it is reduced to clay again.

In all these stages, it was always clay, nothing but clay, only the form changed.

Time is divided into three divisions, which, when reduced, mean only one undivided time.

It is all one road, the part of the road that we have travelled, is the past; the part of the road that we are travelling, is the present; the part of the road that we must travel is the future.

In the same way, age determines childhood, youth, and old age; but there is no age, as there is no time and no form.

There is distraction, there is attention; the two fights; concentration is the result.

There is ignorance, Tamas, there is passion, Rajas, there is purity, Sativa, the three fight - they have fought before, they are fighting now, they will fight hereafter; in the case of the yogi, he controls them all, attains illumination, it is a fight to the finish.

Those who do not carry the fight to the finish are born again and again." Aphorisms of Yoga.

This illumination, or level of heightened concentration, can only be reached through focus exercises and dancing is another activity for developing this skill.

Most cultures have their own traditional dances and some religions, like Sufism in Islam, include dance as part of their worship. These cultural and religious dances allow the dancer to bring their body, mind, and soul into harmony with the rhythm of the music so they can experience joyfulness. Notice how little children love to dance. The music brings a feeling of happiness into their heart and soul freeing them from all inhibitions. Confucius, the great Chinese philosopher urged all young people to devote their time to the arts, especially music and dance, because he said it helped to build the perfect character.

Listening to and reading stories, is another great way to develop concentration. As a child it was my favourite way of withdrawing into my Self.

One story that stayed deep in my memory is, The Little Match Girl.

Once, in a town in Denmark, on the very last evening of the year, New Year's Eve, the snow began to fall, and it became bitterly cold.

Through the cold and gloom walked a little girl; both her head and her feet were bare for she was extremely poor. It is true that she had had a pair of shoes when she left home that morning, but they were her mother's and so were much too big for her. They had slipped off as she ran across the road to dodge two speeding carriages. So now the little girl walked barefoot through the snow. Her feet were sore and red raw with cold. In her hands she was carrying a small bundle of matches and there were a good many more matches in her tattered apron pocket. Nobody had bought any all day long or given her so much as a penny. Cold and hungry, she walked on through the city.

Snowflakes fell on her long fair tresses that curled in pretty ringlets on her shoulders, but she did not notice them. As she walked, she looked in the lighted windows of the houses she passed. The smell of roast goose came to her from several homes. Many families were celebrating New Year's Eve together.

In a narrow alley between two great houses, she sat down, tucking her tiny bare feet beneath her. It did no good; she could bring no warmth back to her toes. She did not dare go home, for she had sold no matches, earned no money and she was afraid her father would beat her.

Besides, her home was not much warmer than the street. She lived in an attic beneath a broken roof, and the wind whistled through it, even though they had tried to block the biggest holes with bits of straw. Her little hands were numb from cold. Perhaps, she thought if she lit a match, it might warm them. If she but dared! Well, she did. She drew one out and struck it against the wall of the house. Oh, how warm it was and how brightly burned the match, just like a tiny candle.

She cupped it in her hands. How funny! She fancied she was sitting before a big iron stove with a fire blazing inside it. How beautifully warm it was! She poked out her toes so that they too could have some warmth. But, alas, in that instant, the flame died, the stove vanished, and she sat alone with a burnt match in her hand.

She lit another. Its flame lit up the wall and somehow made it transparent like a veil, so that she could see right through into the house. She saw a table spread with a snow-white cloth and set with the very finest china dishes. In one dish was a roast goose stuffed with apples and delicious plums. Then—lo and behold—the goose and the knife and fork jumped down from the table and came waddling towards her. The little girl stretched out her arms, but the match went out, and her hands touched instead the cold hard wall beside her.

She struck a third match. It flared up, and by its light she saw that she was sitting under a lovely Christmas tree. It was even grander than the ones she had seen on Christmas Eve through the windows of the wealthy merchants' houses. Hundreds of candles burned on its green branches, and bright little figures like those she had seen in toyshop windows looked down upon her.

She smiled and reached towards them in delight. But at that moment the match went out and she saw that the candles on the Christmas tree were only bright stars in the sky.

One star fell, its trail blazing a line of fire across the sombre heavens.

Someone is dying, murmured the little girl sadly. For her granny had told her that a shooting star was a human soul on its way to heaven.

She struck another match against the wall and in its light, she saw her granny, the only person in her life who had been kind and loving to her. Her granny had been dead these two years past. Yet now she was there, stretching out her arms to the little match girl. "Granny," the little girl cried out, "please takes me with you. I know you'll leave me when the match goes out, just like the nice warm stove, the waddling goose and the lovely Christmas tree!" Hastily she lit all the remaining matches in her bundle lest her granny disappear. The matches burned with such a bright, strong flame that night became as light as day. Never, the child thought, had her granny looked so happy.

Then her grandmother took the little girl in her arms and flew up with her to where there is no more cold, no more hunger, no more pain.

In the cold glimmer of the morning someone found the little match girl curled up in the narrow alleyway. She had frozen to death on the last night of the old year.

The sun of a new year now shone down upon her lifeless body; her lap was filled with burnt-out matches.

Hamlyn Publishing 1986

Now focus your mind on this poem by Mary Stuart so that you can be an instrument of light to all those who are suffering from despair. Meditate and reflect on it so that its message will help to overcome those occasional thoughts of selfishness:

Keep me 0 Lord from all pettiness.

Let me be large in thought, and word, and deed.

Let me leave off self -seeking and have done with fault finding.

Help me put away all pretence, that I may meet my neighbour face to face without self-pity, and without prejudice.

May I never be hasty in my judgments, but generous to all, and in all things.

Make me grow calm, serene and gentle.

Grant that I may realise that it is the trifling things in life that create differences; that in the higher things we are all one.

And O Lord God, let me not forget to be kind.

Developing the higher mind, compassion, forgiveness, calmness and gentleness is not an easy task, especially when the normal pattern of our life gets disrupted in any way.

This happens sometimes when living with teenagers, because unfortunately some teenagers tend to display more of their negative characteristic traits within their families than the positive.

As parents we need to focus on the positives, and to refrain from regurgitating the negative behaviour because that will only increase the threshold of stress and disillusionment within our teenagers and ourselves.

For successful meditation to occur we must aim to keep the mind clear and peaceful under all circumstances, so bear in mind that bringing up teenagers is just a transitory phase in everyone's life.

During my time of living with teenagers I read "Your Child and the Zodiac' by Teri King so that I could get a better understanding of my sons' personalities.

The positive characteristic traits went like this: 'The Scorpions world is one of power and this individual's highest achievement is the manifestation of that power in the most tremendous of tasks, namely complete self-mastery. Scorpions attempt to destroy egotism, to dominate desire, and expel everything that can retard moral, mental, and physical regeneration.'

These words were extremely uplifting when I investigated the distant future for my Scorpio teenager!

And the flip side of his character said: "The negative Scorpio is secretly delighted when he uncovers a weaker or more fallible being, and he will generally proceed quite ruthlessly to express the other's faults to those around. Try putting this type in his place and he will erupt and burn like a volcano. In this case, run for cover before the lava begins to pour forth."

And when my Scorpio teenager behaved like this, I ran for cover and meditated, because I knew that one day, he would beat these negative character traits and a metamorphosis would take place.

For my other son when I read: "This Virgo recognises at a glance the value of other people and treats them accordingly. Feelings reveal themselves in day to day small, thoughtful actions.

They dedicate themselves to work, very often for inadequate pay, finding more satisfaction in helping others," I felt uplifted.

And during the difficult times these words were reassuringly true,

"Others frequently admit they are in the wrong with this character, to, hopefully, find some peace and quiet. This type can be very trying. He has a dogged belief that no one can do things as orderly or as efficiently as he, and this type will drive others mad with an insistence on promptness. This type can be a genuine pain in the neck, who sees himself as a saint."

And I felt further comfort when I read the note on the first page, 'To three wonderful kids Deborah, Justin and Lindsay; and to all parents who retained their sense of humour through parenthood." [Angus and Robertson: 1980]

Whenever we acquire knowledge, irrespective of its source, we cope better because our conscious mind understands what is going on. Confusion arises from our misunderstanding of a situation.

Always bear in mind that a focused well-balanced parent is the best thing any teenager can have. And meditate often when bringing up teenagers because through meditation we can connect to their soul and the energy that goes out to them through our thoughts connects, unconsciously, with their minds. Therefore, it is crucial not to harbour negative or unhappy thoughts about them, because worry and verbalizing those concerns manifests itself in the prolonged action of negative behaviour. Instead, help them to expand their conscious mind through mental pursuits, because the acquisition of knowledge is the greatest of all achievements.

By this I mean all knowledge, whether it is intellectual or creative, but beware of over-taxing the mind with too many hobbies or interests.

And above all, try to nurture their soul through encouraging them to meditate on the good values in life, like thankfulness and appreciation. Even if your child succumbs to the drug scene, always remember that, regardless of their age, they are your children, and if, for whatever reasons communication between the two of you breaks down, you must stay bonded to them spiritually. Admittedly there is a lot of humiliation and pain to bear with drug-addicted children; but we must never deny the strength of our internal energy to strengthen us in all circumstances.

Saint Paul said "When people sin, you should forgive and comfort them, so they won't give up in despair. You should make them sure of your love for them."

Do not focus on the drugs or on the harm it is doing them but instead reach out and get as much support as possible from others. Never try to hide the dilemma and battle on alone, because it could lead to further blockages of the chakras through denial and perhaps to more humiliation when the situation becomes known. Remember secrets do not stay secrets forever.

Once they gain control of their mind, they will resist the once tempting offer of drugs.

At this stage refrain from saying or doing anything that will be detrimental to their fragile state of mind; remember they have gone through a lot in reconditioning their mind and body and the last thing they need to visualize are images from their past. So, forgive and let go.

When we insist on living in an ever-present past; when we refuse to let go, we are behaving like the little spider monkey that refuses to let go under any circumstances.

For years people wanted to study the behaviour of the Spider Monkey, but they were unable to catch this very quick, tiny animal because it was way too fast for tranquilizer guns and nets. Then, one day, a researcher placed a clear, narrow-mouthed, glass bottle with one peanut inside in their natural surroundings and 'zap' he had caught a Spider Monkey.

How did this happen?

Well, when the Spider Monkey put its tiny hand into the bottle and took hold of the peanut its clenched fist could not come out of that bottle. The tiny monkey was not going to let go of the peanut. And because the bottle was too heavy for the monkey to run off with it, it just sat there, with its clenched fist in the bottle. Even when the researcher approached with his net it allowed itself to be caught rather than let go of the peanut!

When we focus on releasing all painful thoughts with love, we will slowly see that all experiences are a step towards our own Self-realization, the light at the end of the tunnel.

Change emotions of anger into thoughts of how to change current situations and work on creative ideas, whether they eventuate or not does not matter, because they generate a new and vital energy called enthusiasm, in comparison to feelings of hopelessness, that stop the soul from evolving. Buddha gave his followers three Universal Truths:

The first one stated that: everything in life is impermanent and constantly changing.

The second was that: because nothing is permanent, life is unsatisfactory.

And thirdly that: even if someone achieves a state of contentment it will not last!

Do not see this as the hopelessness of living but instead see it as the joyfulness of living because every time we jump over a hurdle, we have jumped one more hurdle towards the evolution of our soul because we always experience an expansion of consciousness after a crisis.

When we let go of our bad experiences, we free the mind; hanging onto the aftermath of a crisis holds the mind in a vicious grip and there is no room for expansion.

Think of it as giving birth; the crisis is the labour but once the baby is born there is relaxation and joy. Now what would happen if the mother hung onto the afterbirth?

The labour pain would continue with the pains become more excruciating, until eventually the whole body would be affected and could even cause death.

This is what happens to our mind when it hangs on to something painful, instead of relaxing and enjoying the feeling of relief because the crisis is over it stays locked in with the painful and destructive thoughts of the crisis.

Shri Patanjali, in his Yoga Sutras, third century B.C. said: "The finer afflictions disappear as mind disappears in illumination. The grosser afflictions disappear through meditation."

When we focus our mind on the bright side of life all the nasty side-effects of our experiences will be dissolved and our mind will be illuminated.

Remember, our focus must always be towards the light; the sunny side, for healing to take place.

This process of discarding and selecting thoughts, some of which have been with us since childhood, gives us the opportunity to embrace the truth.

So, think of all experiences as learning experience for our spiritual growth and move away from situations that cause injury to our self-respect because we want our soul to evolve not regress. This journey takes a lot longer when we must make up for lost time on this earthly plane due to the foolishness of our actions.

Some might consciously use divine guidance; others might need the inspiration of other people and for some it could entail a bit of both, so long as our focus does not wander our footsteps will not flounder.

Spiritualists say that we have evolved further spiritually as a collective nation of people because we now have a greater knowledgeable awareness of those actions that are harmful to life on this planet. Undoubtedly millions of people are continuing with their destructive behaviour, even though they are aware of the ramifications of these negative actions.

It is up to all of us who have consciously distanced ourselves from harmful behavioural patterns to stop those actions that obscure the flow of the super conscious energy of the divine, into the human soul.

The greater our focus on the wellbeing of all life on this planet, the greater our own wellness. Bhawan Shri Patanjali said, "Success is immediate where effort is intense."

Remember – where the mind goes, the energy flows!

The success is the transformation from negative to positive in all our life experiences.

If your lifestyle is not giving you optimum health and well-being focus on changing your life.

When seeking change for the better say these affirmations, they are supported by Biblical verses. First ground your feet by standing firmly on the floor barefooted, tighten your legs and bottom, now image roots growing from your feet and going deep into the ground, see the roots spread out from the front, sides and back of your feet. Imagine an enormously powerful root system, that nothing can knock over going down deep, deep into the earth. Now say this affirmation

I am safe.
(The Lord will protect my feet from stumbling and falling)
My life is in harmony.
(All things work together for those who are in Christ)
The Universe protects me.
(If God is for me none can stand against me)
My time is well spent.
(To everything there is a season and a time for every matter)
I have abundance in my life.
(Christ came so that we might have abundance)

Buddha said: "Suffering means not only the pain which people suffer; it also means all those things which make life less than perfect."

Ill health certainly makes our lives less than perfect. When illness strikes, we need to constantly switch our focus from illness to wellness.

Recently, a little four-year old girl accidentally drank some caustic -soda, the internal burns were so horrific that her entire stomach and oesophagus had to be removed. Yet her recovery from surgery was remarkable which the paediatric doctor put down to the child's mental attitude.

Dr Currie said, "Kids don't think about being sick. They just want to get out there and play. That's the best fighting spirit there is."

Always keep in mind that nothing should compromise our good health.

So many people overwork their bodies to make more money, which only leads to the depletion of that wealth when trying to address and cure their ill-health later.

During the twentieth century colossal changes have occurred in our lifestyle.

We have gone from cars that travelled at 6 km/hr to one that can go 1019.4 km/hr, jet powered Rolls Royce Avon 302; from the postal service to the internet and from the telephone to fibre optics long range communications and the mobile phone; and travelling into space.

Today the decisions our mind must make over the vast assortment of choices placed before us are enormous and add to this the many roles everyone is trying to play to the best of their ability has led to a high level of mental tension. When the whole nervous system is tense, we get stress.

Eastern yogis and western psychologists say this is one of the greatest drawbacks of our modern lifestyle.

Sadly though, a lot of this stress is linked to breakdowns in relationships, which causes untold sufferings to the couple and their children and, if not dealt with amicably, can lead to blockages of the Svadisthana and Anahata chakras.

Before committing to any relationship, spend time meditating, this will clear the mind and allow you to see the long-term picture without illusions.

Once the commitment is made the aim must always be to keep the relationship 'strong and healthy'—in other words it should fulfil each person's needs through Faithfulness.

This is when both people protect each person's self-respect.

When couples focus on faithfulness in a relationship, they will eradicate the word blame from their partnership and replace it with responsibility, with each person accepting responsibility for their own welfare and happiness.

Remember we must know our own self first before we can have a successful relationship with another. This releases the feeling of bondage that one person feels when the other doesn't want to take responsibility for events and circumstances that occur in their lives and would rather blame someone else.

A couple should be bonded in their mutual love and respect for each other without any trace of bondage. Through focusing on the good in the partnership and the truthful, unembellished nature of their partner, a couple will enjoy the fruits of a happy relationship, with the added blessing of the evolution of two souls.

Dr. Narayan Dutta says, "A marriage is a partnership in which the husband and wife contribute to the good of all humankind."

In the Ramayana, one of the sacred texts of Hinduism, the epic tale of Rama, an avatar god of pure goodness, was told to the people to give them an insight into the moral and ethical qualities of how committed relationships should be.

Rama personified all the qualities of noble manhood tenderness, honesty, loyalty, and integrity. While Sita, his wife displayed the ideal image of Indian womanhood kindness, gentleness, and truthfulness.

There were approximately 24,000 Sanskrit couplets depicting their life together, which included their marriage:

'Softly came the sweet-eyed Sita, Bridal blush upon her brow,
Rama in his manly beauty came to take the sacred vow.
And a rain of flowers descended from the sky serene and fair,
and soft celestial music filled the fresh and fragrant air.'

Sita went to live with Rama in his father King Dasharatha's palace, both being under the assumption that after the King's death Rama would become King. So, Rama and Sita began married life full of contentment and joy awaiting his preordained destiny. But it was not to be, because the King banished Rama from his kingdom. This was due to a promise he had made to his second queen many years earlier to remove Rama from the palace and make her son the King instead.

But the King, who loved Rama dearly, could not bear to tell Rama the reason for his banishment, so instead he said that he required Rama to pay penance for his killing of a young boy, accidentally, in the jungles. Sita refused to let Rama leave on his own and followed him through the jungles:

'On a bed of leaf and verdure, Rama and his Sita slept,
And the stars their silent lustre, on the weary exiles shed.
And on wood and rolling river, night her darksome mantle spread,
Morning dawned, and far they wandered, by their people loved and lost,
Drove through grove, and flowering woodland, rippling rill, and
river crossed.'

One day, after many months of travelling, Rama and Sita came across the hermit couple in the jungle whose son the king had accidently killed. They told Rama that his father had already paid his dues by building a temple on the spot where their son had been killed in memory of him as retribution. Rama knew now that there were other reasons for his banishment from his father's kingdom, but he continued his wanderings hoping that one day his inheritance would be returned to him.

Now in the vicinity of that jungle lived another King, Ravana, and his beautiful sister who upon seeing Rama fell in love with him and tried everything within her power to steal him away from Sita. But Rama ignored her and remained faithful to Sita which infuriated Ravana's sister and so the two of them decided to kidnap Sita when she was on her own in the jungle.

This they did one day when Rama had wandered away from their hut leaving Sita on her own. Bound and gagged, Sita conveyed her thoughts to the animals and the birds as she was taken away.

'Whisper to my righteous Rama when he seeks his homeward way.
Speak to Rama that his Sita ruthless Ravana bears away.
Ah my Rama, true and tender, thou hast loved me as thy life.
From this foul and impious Raksha thou shalt still revere thy wife.'

Smitten with grief Rama searched high and low for Sita, and one day some of the original inhabitants of the jungles, described as monkey people, found Rama, and told him they had news of Sita's whereabouts. So, Rama, with the leader of the monkey inhabitants, Hanuman, set off for the island of Ceylon where Sita was exiled in a mangrove because she had refused the advances of Ravana. When Rama approached Ravana, he refused to release Sita, so a battle began between Rama and Ravana. Finally, after a fierce and long battle, Rama, helped by his monkey-like warriors rescued Sita and together they fled back to the north of India.

However, they had yet another crisis to overcome. Before Rama could take Sita back to his kingdom as his wife and Queen, she had to prove her fidelity to Rama while she had lived in Ravana's kingdom. She did this by getting the 'monkey' people to build a huge bonfire through which she said she would walk using the power of the God Agni to prove her faithfulness.

'Not a curl upon her tresses, not a blossom on her brow,
Not a fibre of her mantle did with tarnished lustre glow.
Witness of our sins and virtues, God of Fire incarnate spoke.
Bade the sorrow-stricken Rama back his sinless wife to take.'

After this they travelled back together to Rama's kingdom and to his people.

'Joy, Joy, in bright Ajodhya.
Gladness filled the hearts of all.
Joy, Joy, a lofty music sounded in the royal hall.
Fourteen years of woe were ended.
Rama now assumed his own.

And they placed the weary wanderer, on his father's ancient throne.'

More than 5,000 years ago faithfulness was the focus in a partnership, and it is still the same today. To make the focus on faithfulness more intense, and thereby to make the relationship more meaningful, remember the more we value something the more determined the mind will be to preserve it, but it is necessary to acknowledge this partnership, either through marriage or other type of mutual consent. This act of recognition strengthens the emotional and spiritual areas of faithfulness.

Right throughout the age's marriage ceremonies have taken place to try and demonstrate the spiritual aspect of the union. It is not simply two people coming together, but also two souls coming together so that their personalities can evolve to a higher level of consciousness.

It indicates that during that time on earth these two souls have made a bonding commitment to join so they can spiritually grow.

Some Hindus believe that this arrangement was preordained before these souls came to earth so the ceremony becomes a symbolic action between the human-will and the Divine-will.

It shifts into the realm of something sacred, with the ties binding the couple in spirit and in body.

Today's marriage ceremony usually entails a priest who will bless the couple and sometimes holy water is sprinkled on them.

In bygone years incense was burnt near the bridal bed to enhance the physical and spiritual union. Gold rings are exchanged and worn on the fourth finger of the left hand. The vein in this finger is larger and is linked to the heart, hence the reason for wearing it on that finger. During the sixth century in Germany the marriage was sealed with a ring, a kiss, and a pair of slippers. The symbolism of the slippers has never been made known to me so allow your imagination to roam!

These words were taken from a 15th century prayer book in York, U.K.

I take ( ) to my wedded wuf, to have and to holde,
fro this day forward,
for better for wore,
for fayrere for fowlere,
in sycknesse and in hele,
tyl dethe us depart.

More recently, in the Christian Book of Common Prayer the words Love, Honour and Obey were the words said by the bride to the groom.

These three words are the epitome of faithfulness.

Love being the faithfulness of unconditional love that can only flow through the energy of the Anahata chakra.

Honour the greatest respect one person can give another and is the embodiment of truthfulness that flows through the energy of the Vishuddha chakra.

Obey implies a willingness to listen and trust. When a wife demonstrates this in her marriage using the energy from the Ajna chakra it comes back to her, and the union is harmonious. When these words are the focus in a marriage the opening of these three chakras will allow the Sahasrara chakra to open to Self-realization.

This is the bride's personality's personal triumph through her marriage, because by giving these attributes of her personality to her husband she becomes even more faithful, truthful, and trustworthy.

And in the same Book of Common Prayer the Groom says that he will Love and Cherish his wife in their marriage.

Cherish, in its ancient Hebrew translation is a total commitment to care for and acknowledge someone else's needs physically, emotionally, mentally, and spiritually. In other words, through the highest level of care the wife would be nurtured in such a way as to grow in all aspects of her personality.

The Love here is unconditional love.

This total commitment by the Groom will lead to the evolution of his soul, with the energy from the Anahata chakra being enhanced through the blessing of Divine Grace.

When we nurture the positive aspects of a person's personality in a partnership, disciples of Buddhism say spiritual enlightenment will come; because a couple will be spreading love and compassion together, the strength of two being more powerful than that of one. But if they go down the path towards the material world their mind will be dominated by material things that will interfere towards achieving Self-realization.

Buddhists say some couples desire to display their combined material possessions as a successful couple is only an illusion. The reality is that conflict occurs when couples tread down this path of materialism because it brings discontentment into the partnership. Because as their greed for material possessions grow, their need for each other will cease to flow.

Many people renew their marriage vows after some years of marriage.

This is a positive step to take because it brings love and trust back to the attention of the mind and becomes an intention of the will.

Dr Narayandutta says that when we live as loving householders, communicating our loyalty and duties to our families, through respect and truthfulness, we become stronger during adversity.

Some years ago, I lived in Bhubaneshwar, India, in a huge house with my husband away most of the time, through work commitments, whilst our sons were living in a boarding-school in Australia.

The house was beautifully furnished, and it had all the necessary modern aapliances.

One day my ayah, maid, said to me, "Memsahib, I feel so sorry for you living in this big house alone most of the time."

She lived with her husband and four children in a one-roomed mud brick cottage with a thatched roof, she cooked all her family's meals on a coal fire on the front porch where a few chickens scratched in amongst a vegetable garden. They all slept on the floor on a mat with almost no material possessions, yet my ayah felt a deep sorrow within her for what she perceived was my state of loneliness compared to her life of togetherness. She overlooked my material possessions as unnecessary and irrelevant to her life-style and considered them to be too high a price to pay for the absence of her family in her day-to-day living.

Whilst living in this ridiculously large house for one person I was confronted with another unusual statement that caused further reflection within my mind about the conditioning of my thoughts and actions that had become stimulated by the merry-go-round life I lived in a progressive society.

Along with my big house, that had a high wall around it to protect it, I had a large garden that needed a full-time gardener to care for it. Hanging over this wall on either side of it grew the most beautiful hibiscus shrub I had ever seen, with its big vibrant yellow and gold flowers blooming all year round. It bloomed so profusely that both sides of the wall used to be covered with those magnificent yellow and gold flowers.

One day I got really annoyed to see a man get off his bicycle and begin to pick some of my flowers. In a very agitated manner I approached him and asked him what right did he have to pick the flowers without my permission? His gentle reply overwhelmed me emotionally.

He said that while he was riding his bicycle on his way to the temple, he saw the beauty of those gold and yellow flowers in the sunlight and decided to pick a few to place in the temple as a thank-you to God. Not wishing to disturb me he had not asked because he did not think anyone would notice a couple of flowers missing when the bush was so full of them.

My focus switched to how important it was to share, and through meditation I felt joy when I saw him take a few flowers the following week to place in his temple.

And then this verse from the Bible came into my mind:

'Have we not all one God? Did not one Creator create us?"

And I was able to see the placing of those flowers in his temple as a blessing for both of us.

Guru Nanak, the religious leader of the Sikhs, said,

"There is neither Hindu nor Muslim, so whose path shall I follow? I shall follow God's path." This belief that we are all the same in the eyes of God leads us towards enlightenment.

Enlightenment comes when the mind is free from ignorance, the root cause of all our fears.

One of the hardest things the mind must deal with is our own immortality, even though we all know we must die someday. Only when we accept dying as the continuation of life will we embrace the fullness of life, then, even during our difficult times, we will see the glass as half full, never half empty.

To further imprint this acceptance of death into our mind use this focus exercise of visualization. Imagine this lifetime as a holiday, bearing in mind that some last longer than others, our preference being for a good, long holiday, knowing that it will come to an end one day.

At the end of our holiday, even though we are sad it is over, we will be glad to return home again, where everything is comfortable and familiar, amongst loved ones we have not seen for a while. Now, just as we think about our earthly home whilst on holidays, we need to think of our spiritual home whilst we are on Earth. Imagine it as a heavenly Elysium, in Greek mythology, 'a place of perfect peace, set in a beautiful sunlit landscape, illuminated by dancing beams of molten silver.'

And as we go deeper and deeper into this visualization all thoughts of the fear of death will be eliminated from the mind.

When we look at death as returning home from a holiday on Earth, it will never be seen as something to fear and when it is our time to leave the mind will peacefully accept it as a natural conclusion to our holiday. And when we accept death as a normal part of our life the mind will be able to accept the death of others, who are close to us, as normal too. Never focus on the sadness of leaving our loved ones behind; always think of it as a temporary physical separation.

These words, by Cannon Scott Holland (1871-1918), gives us a clear picture of how to view death:

> 'Death is nothing at all ...I have only slipped away into the next room. I am I and you are you ... whatever we were to each other, that we are still.'

Call me by my old familiar name; speak to me in the easy way which you always used.

Put no difference into your tone; wear no forced air of solemnity or sorrow.

Laugh as we always laughed, at the little jokes we enjoyed together.

Play, smile, think of me, and pray for me.

Let my name be ever the household word that it always was. Let it be spoken without effort, without the ghost of a shadow on it. Life means all that it ever meant. It is the same as it ever was, there is unbroken continuity. What is this death, but a negligible accident?

Why should I be out of mind because I am out of sight? I am waiting for you, for an interval, somewhere extremely near, just around the corner. All is well.'

When the idea of death enters our mind, our focus must always be on these three last words-

'All is well.'

Because this is how it is for the ones who have passed over and for those left behind- All Is Well.

Unfortunately, a lot of people view death as something terribly negative an instantaneous drop into the 'fires of hell and damnation'. Totally eradicate this non-sense from the mind.

We know from numerous accounts of Near-Death Experiences, that the person experiencing death feels nothing but light and peacefulness, so images of torture and suffering are senseless; in other words, they make no sense at all when compared with the recorded accounts of NDE.

With meditation, the extended and luminous self will show us the truth, then all dark thoughts about our soul, and the fear of death will be destroyed from the mind, and we can live out our lives joyfully, like in these words of a Christian hymn:

"This is the day, this is the day, that the Lord has made, that the Lord has made, we will rejoice, we will rejoice, and be glad in it, and be glad in it."

When my friend's daughter died, she felt the pain of the physical separation immensely, particularly because she had not had the opportunity to say good-bye.

Then one night, while she lay in her bed in that dream-like state, she felt the distinctive silent presence of her daughter near her, who enfolded her in her arms and said,

"Now mum, this is really good-bye."

My friend was left with a feeling of immense peacefulness because even though she still felt sadness at the physical separation from her daughter, this experience left no doubt in her mind that all was well with her daughter.

We too can have wonderful spiritual interaction with our departed loved ones when we let go of the human pain of death and visualize it as a continuation of the joy of life. When we focus our thoughts to see (using the inner eye) our departed loved ones as beings of light, guiding and helping us on earth, we will feel their presence and their physical absence will be less painful. Christians see death as the resurrection (the rebirth) of the spirit,

Jews and Muslims see it as a journey into the spiritual realm, and Hindus see it as a continuous cycle of birth, death, and rebirth – reincarnation.

In the Bhagavad-Gita Lord Krishna explains the Hindu belief of death:

'I have been born again, and again, from time to time,
To protect the righteous,
To destroy the wicked,
And to establish the Kingdom of God,
I am reborn from age to age.'

Hindus even invented the board-game of snakes and ladders to explain the process of reincarnation. Coming down to earth is represented by the symbol of the snake and going up to heaven, again and again, by the ladder. Each time we come down the snake, we are returning to earth for another lifetime here, and each time we go up the ladder we are returning to our Heavenly home to experience the love and joy in the Heavenly realm, where we go to R.I.P. (rest in peace)

The Buddhists also believe in reincarnation and use mindfulness, going from the conscious mind into the super conscious state through meditation, when choosing their spiritual leader who must be an incarnation of a previous Dalai Lama. These spiritual teachers are so spiritually evolved that at the time of death, and sometimes long before, they can access information from the super conscious mind as to the precise nature of their re-birth. In other words, their conscious mind can receive all the knowledge of where, when and what their next life on earth will be.

This information is recorded by the lama and made known to others after their death with amazing accuracy.

Dr Ian Stevenson, a professor of psychiatry at the University of Virginia, has studied the stories of thousands of adults and children on reincarnation.

One of the most accurate stories was about Corliss Chotkin, a Tlingit Indian man, who said he was the reincarnation of his grand uncle, Victor Vincent. Before Victor Vincent died, he told his niece that he would return as her son with marks on his nose and back like those he had received after an operation. Young Corliss had these birthmarks and from the age of two was able to recall stories and experiences about his grand uncle's life.

Today the Catholic Church is looking further into the belief of reincarnation using these words of Saint Peter as the basis for their study.

"We know that Christ (Jesus) being raised from the dead, will never die again."

In India the subject of death has always been openly accepted, unlike some western cultures where even thinking about it was taboo.

Today adults, and even children, spend a lot more time with the dying, as it is no longer just the domain of the medical and nursing profession; and when death comes it can be more acceptable, with the mind adjusting to the pain of physical separation sooner.

Focus on truthfulness when speaking to children after a death, whether they are people or pets. Stories of 'the bird 'flew away' are dishonest if the bird actually died, the answer 'has flown away to heaven' can be a more truthful description, keeping in mind the understanding and comprehending ability of the child.

Death of a loved one can lead one to immense spiritual growth for the person who is grieving provided they do not allow their mind to wallow in their grief, when this grieving becomes an addiction because it refuses to let go. Remember our thoughts become more deeply connected to those in the spiritual realm after death so constant crying and sadness on our part works against their spiritual peace.

When our focus alters from one of sadness and despair to one of peace the sixth chakra will open fully, like the lotus flower in full bloom, and through our sixth sense, Anja chakra, we will perceive things from beyond the grave.

Some years ago, I received this message from the other side.

One night, whilst in a dream-like state, I saw some documents flash before my eyes with lightning speed and then I was looking under a table at a box with a large red strip on it with the word recipes written in bold print on the top. Whilst I was seeing these things, I felt the presence of my deceased friend Ian, beside me. So, the next morning I phoned his wife and asked her whether she had been looking for some papers. She sounded surprised and said,

"Yes, I've been up most of the night looking for last year's tax assessment papers which I cannot find anywhere and I'm getting really distressed as I have to see my accountant today."

I told her about my vision and suggested she look under a table into a box that had a red strip on it with the word 'recipes' written on the top.

When she returned to the phone, sobbing, she quietly said, "Thank you, I have found them," and then went on to explain how her husband must have placed them there during their recent move before his sudden death. He was the only one who knew where they were, in a place where she would never have thought to look!

This experience gave me tangible proof of our ability to communicate with those in the spiritual realm.

An elderly lady told me that once while in her kitchen her husband appeared near the doorway, he had been dead almost 10 years, looking ever so nice and said,

"What, no tea?" as he had done right through their married life whenever he wanted a cuppa. She had him there with her for an instance large as life.

Then the next day she received the dreadful news that her son was dying on the other side of the country. The appearance of her deceased husband, I believe, was to show her his love and support before she received her heartbreaking news, and to say to her "Don't worry, I'll take care of him when he gets here."

When heartbreak and pain engulf us every new thought that gives us hope must be extended by the conscious mind to lessen the pain of grief.

This simple exercise has helped scores of grieving people.

Write down the birth date of your departed loved one—numerology is the most ancient science in the world—and a person's date of birth is incredibly significant during their earthly life.

For example, if 28.10.1971 was your loved one's date of birth add the numbers together, 2+8+1+0+1+9+7+1=29, next add 2+9=11, then add 1+1=2. Add 0 to this number.

Indian rishis gave great importance to this digit which they called shoonya and linked it to the Om sound and our connection to the Universe.

The number, in this case 20, becomes their spiritual number. Use it for anything that comes up in your life as a lucky number.

Another way of coping with grief and other issues that trouble the mind is to become aware of your dreams because they can be an amazing source of comfort and insight.

W H. Auden said, "Learn from your dreams, what you lack."

Using dreams to tap into the super conscious mind has been around since the beginning of time. Factual evidence of dreams and their interpretations date back to the Babylonians. Ancient Greek and Roman literature are full of references to dreams.

Artem Dorus (140AD) says, "Dreams and visions are infused into men for their advantage and instruction." He believed that the main function of dreams was to enable us to discover the Truth. A truth was revealed to me in a significant way during a time when I had many conflicting thoughts about other religions such as, did all faiths worship the same God?

Then one night I had this beautiful dream.

My husband and I, whilst out driving, saw a lot of people at St. Cuthbert's church, a little old church tucked away in the hills. I thought it was some special service I had forgotten about so I told my husband to stop the car so I could check what was happening.

When I arrived at the door it was wide open, three times its normal size.

I looked inside and there, standing up at the altar was our Christian minister, along with a Hindu priest, a Buddhist monk, a Jewish Rabbi, a Sikh, and three others, whom I knew were from other faiths, but I could not recall which religious faith they belonged to.

I stood at that door for a long time with a feeling that the Truth had been revealed to me.

From that moment on there has never been a shadow of a doubt in my mind that all faiths are reaching out to the same Divine Source of energy.

I now understand that even though our paths might be different our destinations are the same.

No one path is better than the other, and no one's leaders or followers are better than the others; we are simply fulfilling our spiritual journeys in different ways.

There is so much we can learn from dreams and once we learn to master dream-recall and interpretation we will master listening-in to messages from the spirit realm during our waking hours too.

Lynn Andrews, who is part native -American, received this message from her departed mother, 'My daughter, the gateway to death is a strange gateway.

The will of the Great Spirit is the only power that allows passage.

As I once gave you birth, as once you were inside, now you give birth to me, as I am forever within you'.

Doris Stokes, a well-known British medium wrote about the predictions that came to her unbidden and later proved to be true in her book, Voices in My Ear.

And Annie Kirkwood who lives in America has written about the messages she has received from the Blessed Mother Mary. She said they were communicated to her through the mind as internal hearing.

Joan of Arc (1412-1431) received many messages and visions during her short time on Earth. From a young age she would spend long hours in the church kneeling in prayer and meditation, then later, at about the age of thirteen, she became aware of spiritual voices and visions.

She said at first it was simply a voice, as if someone had spoken quite close to her, then she would see a blaze of light and angels would appear.

Sometimes she recognized these angels as St. Michael, St. Margaret, and St. Catherine.

Her voices told her that France and their King, Charles VII were in great danger of being overthrown by the English and the Burgundians.

But when she took her message to the King's commander, he dismissed her as a crazy visionary. A few days later, when the French army was defeated outside Orleans, her visions became believable, and she was taken into the presence of Charles VII.

When the King sought proof of her psychic powers her voices revealed a secret that had bothered the King for a long time. Joan whispered to the King that he had been legitimately conceived and that he could set his mind to rest.

The King was astonished at this revelation for there was no possible way she could have known his secret, except through supernatural means.

Joan also revealed to the King where an ancient sword was buried that no one was even aware of. She said that it was behind the altar in the chapel of St. Catherine-de-Fierbais.

To everyone's amazement it was found in the very spot that her voices indicated.

In April 1429 she told the King that Orleans would be saved and that he would be crowned at Reims soon after. This visionary prediction soon came to pass when in May the English forts which encircled the city were captured and in July 1429 Charles VII was solemnly crowned at Reims.

But despite all the support she gave the King through her visions he did nothing to help her when she was taken prisoner and convicted by the Bishop of Beauvais as a witch and a heretic. Throughout her trial she refused to discuss the voices she heard or describe the appearance of angels, except for saying, "'I saw them with these very eyes, as well as I see you."

Her death was cruel and sad. She was burned at the stake holding a cross close to her heart and calling on the name Jesus.

Twenty-four years later the Holy See called for a revision of her trial and reversed and annulled the previous sentence stating that her voices were Divinely inspired.

In 1909 she was beatified as the Saint of Orleans.

The vision Caedmon an English poet experienced, (670A.D) changed his life forever.

He was born a dumb mute. Every evening, when the people from his village gathered to take turns in singing or reciting poetry, Caedmon would leave and sit quietly in the nearby hills because he felt embarrassed that he could never participate in the singing or poetry reciting.

One evening, while he was sitting alone on the hillside, he saw a presence near him, and a voice gently asked him to sing and miraculously he began to sing.

From that day on he wrote and recited poetry better than anyone else in the village.

The great orchestral conductor, Dennis Gray Stoll said,

"Angels can always speak to us and sometimes when necessary for our spiritual growth will allow us to see them in the glory of their luminous bodies."

George Russell, the Irish poet, and mystic had many visions of ethereal beings and said that it was only spiritual blindness that prevented us from seeing what he saw.

In his book, 'The candle of Visions' he recalls one of his first visions.

"I saw a light streaming from a glowing figure.

Light streams flowed down from it as it moved over me."

The Prophet Mohammed, who began the Islamic Faith in 622AD, received visions from the Archangel Gabriel. These visions and instructions were written down in the Koran.

And in the Bible a vision by three of Jesus' followers is recorded like this:

'One day Jesus took Peter, James and John with him and went up to a mountain to pray.

While he was praying his face changed its appearance, and his clothes became dazzling white. Suddenly two men were there talking with Jesus. They appeared in Heavenly glory and talked with Jesus. When the voices stopped, there was Jesus, all alone. '[Matt: 17]

The men his disciples saw talking to Jesus were Moses and Elijah, two Hebrew prophets who had died hundreds of years before.

The Muslim poet Abdul Karim Jili wrote:

Lo I, the perfect man, am the whole-
and the whole is my theatre.
The sensible world is mine.
And the angel world is of my weaving and fashioning.

The perfect man here represents the perfect personality. It is the reshaping of the perplexing psychophysical intricacies of the body, mind, and soul, coming together in harmony to function at a higher state of consciousness. It is the unfolding of the whole human nature towards that evolutionary force in humankind that will carry them towards an already known, in the super conscious mind, state of bliss through the Divine gift of Grace.

The choice is ours when we seek the super conscious mind over the chaotic conscious mind. James, a disciple of Jesus called the early believers, "men of double mind."

When we meditate and clear the mind of all conscious thought a greater understanding and knowledge will come to us. That is how I received my understanding of reincarnation.

Whilst in deep meditation the belief that we all live many lifetimes here on earth came into my conscious mind with absolute clarity and conviction. It seemed as if this knowledge came to me from a source of condensed knowledge within me. It felt like I had always known it; even though, up to that time, my Christian faith had consciously stopped me from believing in reincarnation.

I now accept reincarnation as a natural passage for the evolution of my soul.

I know that each lifetime is lived for that purpose; and my belief in this has enabled me to recall during deep meditation, many experiences of my other lives.

In these past lives I have seen myself as male and female, rich and poor, pious, and frivolous; a dancer in a Middle-eastern country and a holy child in the camp of Moses, thousands of years ago.

These revelations came as perfectly clear experiences as I became one with the other personality. The memory of them is then transferred from my super-conscious mind into my conscious mind so that I can recall them quite vividly, even today.

This revelation has led me to reflect on the Roman Catholic Church's policy on birth control, that was responsible for a cousin of mine having nine children even though her ill health and poor financial situation caused her immense hardship.

Constantly being dependent on others for help and never being able to repay them, no time, and no money, had damaged her self-esteem, but still she clung fervently to her faith, that told her birth control was sinful.

A Carmelite nun reinforced this belief by telling her that whilst she was in prayer and. meditation, she saw many souls waiting to return to earth. Not only was this nun endorsing re-incarnation, but she also told my cousin that spiritually she was doing a great job because she had made it possible for more souls to be re-born.

It is the experiences of these previous lifetimes that give us the ability to connect to people and situations so profoundly during this lifetime because we have experienced it all before.

Use meditation to seek your own answers and to widen your spiritual horizons.

We are all going through an ever-ascending cycle of spiritual development and growth to that supreme level of infinite knowledge.

From the great Indian spiritual classic, the Bhagavad Gita, come these words:

'I am the beginning and the middle and the end, of all that is,
of all knowledge.
I am the knowledge of the soul.'

And the philosopher, Ecclesiastes from the third century BC said,

"God has put eternity into man's mind, so that he cannot find out what God has done from the beginning to the end."

If eternity is not in the conscious mind, how was Ecclesiastes aware of it? He must have acquired it through the super conscious mind.

When we learn how to access this inner wisdom, all our doubts and fears will be released, because of a new Self-confidence.

People who commit suicide do so because they lack faith in their ability to solve issues that are troubling them. They see their situation as hopeless and their mistakes and failures as too big to overcome, so they give up.

When we were living in the United States, we had an opportunity to witness a space shuttle being launched into space—what an awesome experience. Just standing there watching it soar into space made me think how incredible, what ingenuity, how perfect.

And then, not long after, the next space shuttle crashed soon after take-off. And then it was back to the drawing board and lots of hard work to get things right.

Making a wrong right makes us stronger when we use the wisdom and strength from within.

Jesus lived in a time that was not too different from how we live today. The pressures and stresses were simply different. Through his Divine powers he would have known that one of his close companions was going to commit suicide, yet there is no mention in the Bible of Jesus trying to stop Judas from taking his own life. Why? Because Jesus knew that Judas would return to Earth in another lifetime, to learn those lessons of betrayal and self-forgiveness he needed to master, so that his soul could evolve. At a deeper level of consciousness Judas would have known that, with divine mercy, his spiritual strength would have enabled him to move forward and alter those traits in his personality that were weak, so that he could rise above all forms of dishonest behaviour and live a faithful life, but the confusion in his conscious mind stopped him from seeing clearly and gave him just one option, that of suicide.

Most suicide victims leave a note behind and invariably the note will end with, 'I will be back.'

They know at that moment when they choose to return to the spirit world leaving behind unfinished work that they will return to earth to complete those tasks necessary for their soul to evolve. This lifetime, whilst on their journey their wheel got stuck and they did not reach out for human or spiritual help—even though deep within they knew help was available. Nonetheless their journey will continue the other side and once their soul is refreshed and restored, they will return to earth again with their mission being to spread love and gain wisdom.

Like those who commit suicide terminally ill patients who choose euthanasia deny themselves the chance to spiritually evolve further, due to the body and mind being worn out, but their spiritual journey will continue the other side, and in their next life.

Roger Cole says, "Shortening that process is presumably an act of compassion on this side, but probably leaves that soul with something they have to finish when they move into the afterlife."

Cole's experiences with Raja Yoga meditation and its philosophy of the soul are central to his work as a palliative care specialist.

According to the teachings of Raja Yoga "I am soul, and not a body; my original nature was peace, and everything experienced or expressed is a faculty of the soul."

This belief enables Cole to bring a level of spiritual attachment to his relationships with dying people. "In my role as a physician I can offer much needed help with pain control, but I also try to enter each relationship with spiritual awareness. When I succeed in this, I find that I am lighter, more relaxed, and attentive, and more responsive to their suffering. Through self-awareness I automatically sense the eternal nature of others and witness suffering as a temporary phase of spiritual adjustment. This brings a feeling of closeness and empathy, without being distressed or reactive. I find that people will then open up so that I can understand their physical, emotional and spiritual needs more deeply."

Often the suffering of others can save another human life through the research the physicians do on terminally ill patients, and this involuntary act of helping will enhance the soul, and when that person does leave this earthly life, their strength and courage can be an inspiration to others.

This is how I felt when my young friend died from the devastating disease of Aids.

His serene state of mind will remain an inspiration to me forever. From a young handsome man his body wasted away slowly to a pathetic bone structure mostly devoid of flesh and yet he never failed to see beauty around him even when his eyesight started to fail.

His talents were many, so with great pride I honour his memory by asking you to read this poem he wrote, in the hope that someone might also be inspired to plod on, with a strong mind and heart.

'I sat in the park as autumn was in its final chapter.
But a few pages to go.
Retaliating with splendour against the gloom of winter.
Even so—those leaves too frail
Slowly drifted to the ground.
Nature as it discards does it beautifully.
I will go for a walk and drag my feet through the leaves
And hear them crackle.
It will not be long before they are all gone.'
Gerald

So many people have helped us even after their death whether it is monetary or through their talents, or the many ways that they have inspired us to be better people. Our lives have been enriched due to their generosity. From the many people who have come into my life and then passed over to the next life I have learnt that the only way to receive in life is to give.

Sometimes people have said to me how tired they are of helping certain people because they just take and take and never give anything in return? This is not an excuse to stop giving or helping—look around, even though the people you help do not return the favours you will become aware of other people who come into your life and help.

We must never stop giving and we must never stop being grateful for everything good that comes into our life, no matter how small it might be.

Gratitude unblocks the higher chakras, which leads to wholeness (holiness).

This wonderful painting reminds us to be thankful for even the basic things in our life.

A detail from the 1894 painting,
The Thankful Poor by artist Henry O. Tanner

Mother Teresa said, "You have to be holy in your position, as you are, and I have to be holy in the position that God has put to me. So, it is nothing extra ordinary to be holy. Holiness is not the luxury of the few. Holiness is a simple duty for you and for me. We have been created for that." In the Bible we are given another clue towards achieving holiness:

> 'Do not let kindness and truth leave you. Write them on
> the tablet of your heart'. (Proverbs 3:30)

When we practice meditation all the positive aspects of our personality will come to the fore, and we will experience this holiness that leads to enlightenment.

The XIV Dalai Lama, Tenzin Gyatso said,

"The gift of learning to meditate is the greatest gift you can give yourself in this life."

When we combine yoga with meditation we will transcend the ego through the action of endurance, enthusiasm, and concentration.

The Sanskrit word yoga means to 'yoke' together the mind and body. The science of yoga is unique because it encompasses all the types of problems associated with the human condition. Continued practise of yoga completely purifies the ego through the release of the energy from the chakras. Together yoga and meditation seek to create a union between the individual, whose existence is finite, and the Divine, which is infinite.

Doreen Virtue, an author and clairvoyant, received these messages from the Angels about the benefits of yoga – 'the yogic practice is a silent path that enriches you from within.

Those who originally practiced yoga sent prayers forward in time asking that all who afterward conducted yoga would receive those prayers.

When you engage in the practice of yoga you are immersed in the flow of those ancient prayers.'

All the great philosophers of the past and those in the present meditated daily to get greater insight and wisdom.

Saint Cuthbert, a Christian monk who had great spiritual insight remarked, after some learned religious leaders had visited him, that, "They know their alphabet, but cannot read the earth or the sky." This was after they had attempted to return home by boat during stormy weather.

There is a story about Saint Cuthbert who was standing on the seashore in Scotland in deep meditation completely oblivious to everything else around him. In his heightened state of transcendental meditation, he was unaware that the tide had come in and it was not until the icy-cold water reached his neck that his awareness returned, and he walked out of the sea!

A Buddhist lama has stated that we should spend our lifetime, like the Buddha, on a journey towards the truth, not by logic or by being morally righteous, but by methods of meditation and contemplation that purify the soul.

There are many different meditation techniques, but the experiences are all the same, we just need to find one that allows the body to become totally relaxed whilst the soul is awake.

Before his crucifixion Jesus prayed and asked his disciples to be 'watchful' but his disciples went off to sleep instead. Jesus was trying to get his disciples to meditate so that they would have the extra strength to cope with the traumatic experiences of his forthcoming death.

Hindus call this state of watchfulness Samadhi when unimagined power enters the mind and body. Yogis say that during this trance-like state,

'The procession of cause and effect comes to a standstill; the procession of past and present becomes an eternal presence.'

To successfully meditate you first need to learn how to totally concentrate on just one object. Most religions use beads of some sort to help people stay focused.

Catholic Christians have a string of beads called the Rosary, on which prayers are chanted.

Hindus, Buddhists, and Muslims also use beads when they pray and meditate.

And the indigenous people of Australia have sacred stones called teaching stones that are used for spiritual rituals and meditation.

If you do not have a string of beads to focus on use crystals or gemstones because they are an excellent tool for directing the mind to focus on one thing, before going into meditation.

Find a stone that you particularly like and stay focused on it in your hand, do not think of anything else. If a thought enters your mind move it on because thoughts stop the mind from entering that state of nothingness. Only when the mind is empty of all thoughts can meditation occur.

Make each meditation a purpose filled session. Before you start, think about what you would like clarity or help with, if it is purely to rest the mind then let that be your goal but if there is a particular problem that requires solving think about it then let that thought go, as you empty your mind into nothingness.

Like the beads and gemstones, the Tibetan Singing Bowl is excellent for developing focus skills with the bonus of healing. This metal bowl when hit with a wooden stick makes a powerful vibrating sound that vibrates through the body's fluids and massages the delicate tissue cells to create healing. This sound is a lot like the purring sound of cats, that scientists say trigger the healing process in feline bones.

Begin each meditation by saying a prayer or a mantra. This offers our gratitude for the Divine energy that mingles with ours during meditation as expressed so beautifully in this poem.

'Gradually the river grows wider
the banks recede
the water flows more quietly
and in the end
without any visible break
it becomes merged with the sea.'

Some Christians recite the Hail Mary to give them spiritual strength and inspiration.

Hindus and Buddhist chant the Om the most sacred of all the mantras.

Yogis believe that the Om sound is the echo left behind from the Big Bang and that it is the original sound that arose at the time of creation.

The Apostle John made a similar reference to the word, amen when he wrote in Revelation 3:14: 'The words of the Amen, the origin of God's creation. This is the message from Amen. This is the message from the One who has the Seven Spirits of God."

Mystics believe that the Om sound contains the essence of the entire universe because it's three sounds, a—u—m represents the earth, the atmosphere, and the heavens.

It is interesting to note here that people who have had out of body experiences often remember a particular vibrating sound that engulfed them whilst their spirit travelled in space before returning to their human body again.

Betty Eadie, who clinically died after an operation, had such an experience which she recalled in her book Embraced by the Light. In it she writes –

"I heard a pleasant comforting sound that made me happy, it was a tone like a note of music but was universal and seemed to fill all the space around me. The tone produced soft vibrations and, as they touched me, I knew they had the power to heal."

Choose your chant, prayer, mantra, or symbolic actions carefully and say or perform it with reverence before beginning a meditation, because it displays a conscious effort on your part in seeking Divine guidance.

To meditate successfully it is particularly important for the body to be in a comfortable position.

Relax every part of the body by placing your focus on each area in turn, whilst the mind remains calm.

Begin with the feet, feel gratitude well up within you for this part of the body, and allow the feet to relax, feel your feet relaxing by wriggling each toe, then letting it relax, with the mind totally focused on the feet.

Now shift your focus to your legs and feel the strength and energy in the calves and knees, then feel them relax. Now focus on the thighs and buttocks, and feel them sitting comfortably, then sink them further down, totally relaxed.

Next spend time focusing on your back, especially the backbone and say a silent thank you for its support and for the power it gives to the whole body.

If there is any back pain, take your focus to it and feel it getting better through the power of the internal energy. Next contract the muscles of the anus (Mula Bandha) and breathe in deeply from the base of the spine to the top of the head, Sushumna.

Then breathe out down Pingala and Ida, two powerful nadis, nerves, that run on either side of the spine. These two nadis, the male (yang) and female (yin) are aspects of the life-force energy within. Breathe in through Sushumna and out through Pingala and Ida 5x.

Release the Mula Bandh, and now take your attention down to your hands and give thanks for all the work they do. Feel each finger in turn mentally and then give the hands permission to relax. Move up the arms and think of all the tasks they accomplish each day, the fetching, and the carrying and the hugs of affection; and let them relax too.

Now feel the strength in your neck, swallow some saliva and feel it go down the throat; do this a couple of times until the throat muscles relax. Focus on this energy centre (Vishuddha) for a while and send a conscious thought to the brain for added wellness here so the throat can ward off unhealthy bugs.

Then come to your shoulders and feel them relaxing, and now cast all your worries and cares over to the Universe because their burden is Light.

Feel the shoulders relax as they drop in peace.

Now take your awareness to your head and feel it sitting lightly on your shoulders and thank the Divine power for all the wisdom, all the knowledge, all the goodness that is within, and feel that supreme presence within.

Think of the eyelids, gently open, and shut the eyes and imagine the third eye strengthening as you feel a slight stirring of air in this location.

Feel thankful for the eyes and all the beauty they see.

Now imagine rays of luminous light emitting from the top of your head.

Now move the focus to your breath by taking a deep breath in and slowly let it out.

Do this at least five times and then gently return to normal breathing.

Feel it getting slower, and slower, and slower, and with this slow motionless breath, say silently—calm, calm, calm, calm, until the mind is free of all thoughts, and you reach that deepest part of your being where you feel Nothing.

Stay in this very peaceful state for about ten minutes.

Remember, if you doze off it is not meditation, so wake yourself up and try it again. If thoughts enter your conscious mind return to saying—calm, calm till those thoughts are forgotten. When you feel the ten or twenty minutes is up, bring yourself into full awareness by flexing your forgers and toes, then gently open your eyes and gaze softly at an object for a minute or so before physically moving yourself.

Whenever you are feeling down or tired do a five-minute meditation, you will be amazed at how refreshed you feel afterwards.

A relative of mine had been ill for an awfully long time and on this day, she was feeling at her lowest. She forced herself to do a quiet meditation but only felt slightly better after it, so she turned on the radio and it started to play the song 'Over the Rainbow' with the words

'Somewhere Over the Rainbow, Skies are Blue'.

The guidance she had received while she meditated led her to turn on the radio and, in that song, she got a message that lifted her spirits. Then the postman arrived, and she received a card with a rainbow on the front of it!

If it is at all possible join a meditation group because we all learn and grow through interaction with others, find one that is flexible because no-one needs any pressure in their lives.

Even though a sense of commitment is necessary for our personality to evolve to a higher plane, commitments that cause a feeling of guilt when they cannot be attended to are mentally and emotionally damaging.

Sometimes, after practicing meditation, the spiritual urge to be nourished might become stronger, and participating in a religious faith might be the answer. Choose a group that is free from all prejudices and negative thoughts about our fellow human beings. Diversity, not division, allows us to find the truth. Religious groups that seek the truth, which is light and knowledge, will accept human individuality and value the rich diversity that other religions or cultures offer.

So set out 'to seek and ye shall find' the most nurturing environment for your soul.

Whether we meditate on our own or in a group our aim must always be to achieve inner peace. And then this peace will enhance every aspect of our lives.

Today more and more psychologists are recommending meditation to their patients.

They too believe that this is a healthy way of coping with life's difficulties, especially in changing people's attitudes and behaviours.

Remember meditation is simply the art of mastering concentration, the concentration of total nothingness.

People who practise Zen Buddhism spend as much time as they can in meditation.

To improve their focus, they build special gardens that contain different patterns in stone.

People sit around and only focus on these patterns; though most Buddhists believe that almost anything can be a focus, if it distracts one from having lots of conflicting thoughts.

This Buddhist saying from the Dhammapada is what we all need to remember:

'It is you who must make the effort.
The Great of the past only showed the way.'

And this from Bob Marley:

'Emancipate yourself from mental slavery. None but ourselves can free our minds.'

On my travels I read and heard many beautiful stories but this one is one of my favourites and now I feel it sums up everything that I have written in this book.

In one of the picturesque villages in Switzerland there stands the Mountain Valley Cathedral.

Not only is it a truly magnificent cathedral but it also has the most beautiful sounding organ in it.

When it is played, the music echoes right through the valley.

Well, for a long period of time it sat there, out of order.

The church people brought experts from all over the world to repair it, but no one could.

Then one day an old man appeared at the church and said he had heard about the organ being out of order and would like to fix it. For two days the old man worked in almost total silence on that organ, and then got it playing again as beautifully as it had done before.

When the Pastor asked in amazement how the old man had fixed it, he said,

"I built this organ fifty years ago and now I have restored it."

When the Divine energy flows through our energy, we too can be restored to all our glory.

Shanti, Shanti, Shanti, Om
May peace be always with you, in your mind, heart and soul—
from this moment on
And may your leader be your Soul,
And may you,
Follow the Leader.